Annmarie O'Connor is the bestselling author of *The Happy Closet*, a fashion writer and an award-winning stylist. Her editorials and stylings appear in the *Irish Examiner, The Sunday Times Style, The Irish Times, Irish Tatler, Image* and *The Gloss*. Over the years, she has reported from the catwalks of London and Paris and has interviewed fashion figures such as Victoria Beckham, Vivienne Westwood, Matthew Williamson, Manolo Blahnik and Ab Fab's Jennifer Saunders. She is also the editor of the *Louis Vuitton City Guide to Dublin 2012*. She has worked as stylist to the coaches on the *Voice of Ireland*, and has styled shows at London Fashion Week and, closer to home, luxury department stores Brown Thomas and Harvey Nichols.

On air, she is a contributor to *The Dave Fanning Show, The Ryan Tubridy Show*, TV3's *Xposé, Ireland AM* and RTE's *Today Show*. She was featured as one of Ireland's 100 Most Inspiring Women in 2011 and appeared on Ireland's Power List in *Irish Tatler Business* in 2013, 2014 and 2015. In 2015, she was the winner of the Kerry Fashion Week Best Irish Fashion Stylist and the Irish Fashion Ambassador award.

The Happy Medium

Swap the weight of having it all for having more with less

Annmarie O'Connor

Gill Books

Gill Books
Hume Avenue
Park West
Dublin 12
www.gillbooks.ie

Gill Books is an imprint of M.H. Gill & Co.

978 07171 7273 3

Design and print origination by O'K Graphic Design, Dublin

Edited by Ruth Mahony

Printed by CPI Group (UK) Ltd, Croydon, CRO 4YY

This book is typeset in 11/17 pt Minion with headings in Advert Light

The paper used in this book comes from the wood pulp of managed forests. For every tree felled, at least one tree is planted, thereby renewing natural resources.

5 4 3 2 1

The only thing that is immune to change is our desire for meaning.

To my father, who walked the middle path

CONTENTS

INTRODUCTION

The middle ground. It doesn't get much press, does it? There's no click-bait in stability, no hedonic headline in balance, no cliff-hanger in even keel. Hearts don't beat faster, palms don't get sweaty, mouths don't dry up. In fact, we do our level best to avoid its average reputation. Why walk the path of least resistance when there's a sheer rock-face to climb? Because it makes sense to, that's why.

My name is Annmarie O'Connor. You might know me as the author of *The Happy Closet,* or you might not know me at all. Either way, allow me to introduce myself. I'm an inexpert expert on the subject of mindfulness. My first book, *The Happy Closet,* helped readers declutter their wardrobes from the inside out by using positive psychology to clear the hang-ups and habits that shape sartorial well-being. This book, *The Happy Medium,* will help you gain perspective on your personal satisfaction from the outside in by using positive psychology to clear unsustainable expectations of what constitutes a life well lived.

What makes me qualified to riff on happiness? Not a lot. Just my own outlook. I believe that happiness is found on your own terms – not the dictates of the masses or the validation of a crowd. As for me? I'm 43; I'm single; I still rent; I earn less than most of my peers; I had a cat (but he left me); and I still don't know how to drive. By society's standards, I'm invisible; by my standards, I'm rather happy. Admittedly, my life sounds more like a country-and-western song than that of a self-help author but, aside from the packaging, it's exactly what I hoped for as a freewheeling twenty-something (more on that later).

Are you still with me? This is generally where I lose people. No one queues up to hear about the life more ordinary. We've been primed to expect more, aspire to better, nothing less than the best. The speed of modern culture combined with the hyper-connectivity of technology has shifted our perspective from good enough to never enough. With that, the story-making moments of our lives are carefully constructed and edited with social media tools to create blemish-free narratives that always end in a happily ever after. The reality? It's making us miserable.

Think about it: the very concept of 'having it all' carries its own burden. 'All' by its definition suggests 'the whole of'. The whole of what exactly? 'All' is limitless and, to be fair, that's a mighty big ask. Being the inexpert expert that I am, my humble prescription is one of applied mindfulness – a happy medium, if you will. Let's be clear: this isn't a mantra of mediocrity. Rather, it's about finding balance in a full-throttle culture, discovering what it is you need so you can get more of what you want – your very own happy medium.

The best bit? You don't need any fancy equipment, annual subscription or special handshake to get started; there's no diet of chia seeds, crash course in chakra cleansing or mastering a mudra required to identify your sweet spot. Self-awareness starts inside your own head, that sacred space where you can take five, tune into your radar and decide what frequency best suits you. Sometimes our aspirations are as lofty as an unfurling clifftop mansion; sometimes they're as simple as a cup of coffee and a midday nap. Sometimes well-being is, *well*, well enough. And what's so bad with that?

If you'd like to swap the weight of 'having it all' for a more mindful life mantra, then get ready. It's time to discover your happy medium.

CHAPTER 1

Something's Gotta Give

Road to Nowhere

The road must eventually lead to the whole world. Ain't nowhere else it can go – right?

JACK KEROUAC, *ON THE ROAD*

We are storytelling creatures. Even our earliest ancestors sat around fires spinning yarns, painting tales on cave walls and trading tribal titbits. These narratives did more than simply entertain or pass the time; they became our heritage, our identity, our guiding principles. More importantly, they helped us to connect, to form communal bonds with those who shared the same viewpoint and to create plot twists with those who held opposing perspectives. Woven together, their meaning steered our course amid choices and challenges, forming a blueprint for the tapestry of life. Then something changed.

Our cultural compass turned away from the tribe and toward the individual, as a result of the rise of technology, our newly appointed talisman. As old social structures crumbled, a brave new world emerged – one of boundless potential and unlimited options for independence. With each new advance came the renewed promise of ease and freedom. It was now up to us to craft our own stories, to be the author not of who we were or once were, but of who we thought we should be.

Unsure of how to proceed, we looked to others for guidance. 'Be more!' they said. 'Be better! Rise to the top! Rise *over* the top!' But no one really seemed to know where the top was, not even our shiny new gadgets – just that we should get there. With no beginning, no middle and no end in sight, the pressure to be *more* left us feeling *less*. What if the top wasn't the story we wanted to tell? What if our story was somewhere in the middle? What then?

Fearful, we continued our ascent. With so many different routes, the way forward was confusing. Along the way, we met others travelling alone in the same direction. 'How far have you come?' we'd ask. Curious to compare our own progress, we'd look backward and forward, forward and backward, until motion sickness called a brief halt to our journey.

Dizzy with anxiety, we failed to see some folks sitting by the roadside enjoying the view, others stopping for a chat.

Instead, we focused what energy we had on moving ahead, consoling ourselves that we'd get there in the end. There – that magical place where expectation lives, where tall tales are told and happily ever after begins. There. If only we knew where it bloody was.

Is it any wonder some of us feel so lost? Never have we been so liberated, so free to design our destiny, to play the lead character in our lives. Never has decision-making been so exhausting. And therein lies the rub. With a ransom of untold alternatives hanging like a noose around our necks, the expectation stakes just keep getting higher and higher *and higher*.

Thanks to our tablets, smartphones and even smarter watches, the incessant flux of information in our lives mean only the truly exceptional – that 1% – make a significant impact on our conscious awareness. Second best rarely gets a look in. In order to be seen or heard, the onus is on each of us to break the internet, break a record, break wind even – so long as we come first; so long as everyone knows about it. This need to move or improve, to nip or tuck, to upgrade or trade in is more than just a superficial pursuit. Rather, it's a deep-rooted fear powered by our ancestral aversion to losing – the fear of social exclusion, being eliminated, made invisible.

These days, wanting 'enough' has become the equivalent of farting in public: an embarrassing and inadmissible gaffe. In a culture bent on personal agency, enough is never enough, especially when the prospect of reinvention promises so many possibilities. Lost your job? Build an empire! A bit skint? Become a financial ninja! Looking for love? Swipe right until your finger cramps! Just when we start to feel the audible hum of contentment in the ether, some sneaky fecker upgrades the software, leaving us to curse our broadband speed. If only we could find the reset button.

What if we could? What if restoring our factory settings was *that* easy? If we change the definition of happiness from having it all to wanting what we have, finding the middle ground could be less of an epic journey and more of a cake-walk. The key to having more with less? Making the bold decision to be satisfied, to be enough. In order to do that, some holistic housekeeping is in order. We'll get to that a moment. First, let's meet the thought leaders who started this revolution all those years ago: the philosophy majors who put the happy medium on the mind map.

A Short History of Happiness

It's the sides of the mountain that sustain life, not the top.

ROBERT M. PIRSIG, *ZEN AND THE ART OF MOTORCYCLE MAINTENANCE*

This history of happiness is a long story, so I'm going to give you the long story short. Consider it a condensed-milk summation of the subject: concentrated with a proven shelf life and great over coffee. Here's why.

Happiness may appear to be the preserve of the privileged, a New Age nuance or a pastime for those with too much time to think. In reality, it has long been a hot-button topic, one which has served as a social yardstick and moral compass for civilisations from West to East. Far from being the preserve of ladies fist-pumping the sky in tampon ads or yoghurt marketers hawking digestive well-being, its provenance is part of a wider ethical ecology where a mindful attitude is its own reward.

Ancient Greek philosophers, like Socrates, Plato and Aristotle, ushered in a radical discourse on the subject, collectively shaping Western civilisation as we know it. These three fellas basically put the responsibility squarely on our shoulders. No hiding behind divine providence or the flimsy excuse of fate. No siree. The present held all the possibilities for life satisfaction. It was time for us to step up to the plate of self-determination and stop whining about why nobody was feeding us grapes.

Socrates (469–399 BC), chief influencer and seminal tastemaker, was the first to get the ball rolling. His pioneering belief that happiness was achievable with a bit of graft blew a *eureka*-sized hole in the assumption that the gods controlled the gig. Armed with a mix of ethics and no-nonsense practicality, Socrates suggested that a bit of balance can go a long way to keeping us satisfied; in other words, we shouldn't confuse wants with needs. His Socratic method – a precursor to modern mindfulness – focused on exploring the present moment with curiosity and exerting personal influence over one's quota of contentment. Socratic happiness wasn't a magic pill, a jammy inheritance or a birthright – it was a personal achievement.

Plato (428–347 BC), a student of Socrates, delved deeper into the 'virtue', or moral code, of happiness. The Platonic viewpoint positioned happiness as that which enabled people to live good lives. Not to be confused with our contemporary interpretation of the good life (leisure, wealth and pleasure), Plato saw happiness as having a broader social function, a duty to the community and justice – well-being, if you will. Also, this guy had no time for idleness, excess or people with notions. Your granny would've loved him.

Aristotle (384–322 BC), a student of Plato, was a die-hard happy-hunter. In fact, his dedication to the genre would make the Amazon self-help back catalogue look like a pity party. Completing the Greek circle of thought, his teachings co-opted the Socratic belief in personal responsibility while expanding his mentor's definition of the good life to include broader assets like health, wealth, friends and the odd glass of wine. Not that self-indulgence was indulged; quite the opposite. Aristotle believed we all have a happy medium – or what he dubbed 'the mean'. In other words, you wouldn't catch him carousing at a toga party if he had a philosophy lecture in Plato's Academy the next day. Smart thinking.

Meanwhile, in another part of town, Eastern mystics and sages such as Lao Tzu, Buddha and Confucius were preaching a similar ideology, albeit with less hustle, more flow. These guys advocated keeping a keen eye on the 'mean' or 'middle path', while exercising mindfulness, moderation and morality in all aspects of life. Extremes weren't on the curriculum.

Legendary Chinese philosopher **Lao Tzu** (*c.* 601–531 BC) led the charge. Credited with inspiring Taoism and the revered *Tao Te Ching,* an instructional manual on living the good life, his word was gospel. The *Tao,* or 'way', was promoted as the even path to happiness and harmony (the authentic self). To find it, it was necessary to accept and live in unison with what surrounded us. His happiness hack? Practicing *wu wei,* otherwise known as focused attention or 'flowing'. If, as Tzu believed, life's best decisions are made with effortless action, then slowing down to smell the roses ain't such a bad thing. Cancel your 3 o'clock. Life just dropped by.

Buddha (563–483 BC), a.k.a. 'the awakened one', shared Lao Tzu's belief in going with the flow. Born into a wealthy Nepalese family, Buddha awoke to the fact that all of creation is defined by suffering. Far from turning him into a killjoy, his approach to dealing with this revelation was to adopt a lifestyle of moderation or 'The Middle Way'. Like Aristotle, his version of the good life wasn't one of overindulgence or eschewing creature comforts but one of embracing the space in-between. Happiness for Buddha was an inside job generated by the practice of non-attachment, acceptance and perspective. In other words, misery isn't a by-product of whatever first-world problems you've hashtagged on your Instagram account; it's because you need to sort your priorities out.

Confucius (551–479 BC), Chinese teacher, editor, politician, philosopher and rumoured student of Lao Tzu, was one of the East's first self-help gurus. Ever the rebel, he believed we all possessed the power of transformation and bucked the idea of lineage bestowing 'nobility'. His mission statement, *The Doctrine of the Mean*, can be summed up as follows: happiness (or 'virtue') is developed in one's character, not one's circumstances. It fulfils a broader social function or *jen* – a feeling of concern for the well-being of others. Most of all, it never overdoes it. Steady Eddies, rejoice!

Collectively, our happiness-theorising forefathers taught us to do our best, to do right by others and to enjoy the present while keeping an eye on the future – to be satisfied. Simple, right? Maybe not. Somewhere along the way, we confused doing our best with not doing enough, maintaining inner calm with ticking over. Happiness became a moving target, with increased expectations jeopardising our aim. Is happiness a state of being? A state of mind? A bag full of cash, 10 wives, and an S-Class Mercedes? In a world beset by multiple choice, finding that centre-point is no mean feat. So how do we decide what will make us happy? Glad you asked.

Deciding to be Satisfied

Folks are usually about as happy as they make their minds up to be.

ABRAHAM LINCOLN

I remember the excitement. I was 16 years old and proudly brandishing 10 golden scratch-cards in my hand. Grinning gormlessly from ear to ear, I began to get an inkling something was wrong. The stares from well-meaning neighbours said, 'Don't do it, kid!', 'You'll regret it!' Still, I chose to ignore their palpable unease and deliver to my mother the prize she had won at the local community raffle. Let me fill you in. She didn't *win* 10 scratch-cards, per se. I chose them for her (without prior consultation) from a selection of available prizes, including but not limited to a month's supply of coal or briquettes, a tonne of turf, a hamper from the local shop and dinner for two. There was no contest. Why settle for a hot meal or a warm house when you could build a castle (in the air, admittedly)? You get the picture. Much like Jack and his magic beans, I traded a sure thing for a vague promise and got the living bejaysus reprimanded out of me. For the record, she won £4. 'At least we can buy another two scratch-cards,' I offered weakly. Kids – they never learn. Neither do adults, for that matter.

When faced with an adequate reality or the potential of infinite riches, most of us opt for the magic beans … Am I right? Defined as 'to do enough', satisfaction is perceived as the *gateway* to happiness – a minimum entry requirement rather than an end in itself. But there's a bit more to it than that. Let's put this into context.

Satisfaction, a reliable people-pleaser, is often ignored in favour of her hotter cousin, happiness, who, let's face it, is measured by economists, promised by politicians and relentlessly pursued by the masses. She even has her own theme tune (thanks, Pharrell). Them's tough odds.

That said, happiness bears her own burden of expectation: a certain 'have it all' image amplified by her universally-ordained celebrity status. Satisfaction's less Googled reputation makes her vastly underappreciated but also free of public projection. No one expects a lot from the smart yet plain sidekick, which is why she's got the upper hand over happiness.

Consider satisfaction the unsung administrator of your well-being – an ally you would be wise to win over before throwing shapes at Her Highness happiness. Without satisfaction, nothing gets done. Calmer and less intense, she helps focus attention on what matters most. The result? Better decisions. Happiness may be *swit swoo*, but satisfaction – she's *wu wei*. After all, if you're never satisfied, how happy can you really be?

Part of the problem is that we've become promiscuous when it comes to choice. With no true commitment level, we dip in and out of things willy-nilly, never forming an intimate bond with what we really need and thus never knowing what we really want. Instead of cuddling up with satisfaction, we've become hooked on the thrill of the chase, addicted to its toe-curling, albeit brief, climax. The result? Afterwards, we feel a bit empty, as if somehow cheated in the expectation stakes. Don't be too hard on yourself, though. There's a good reason for your bad judgement.

American psychologist Barry Schwartz, author of *The Paradox of Choice: Why Less Is More*, maintains the greater the opportunity pool, the less sure we are of our direction and selection, and the less satisfied we are overall. Worse still, as humans we're scientifically proven to be bad at choosing what will make us happy, as psychologist Dan Gilbert explains in *Stumbling on Happiness. Awfully bad* (see: scratch-cards a.k.a. magic beans). Clearly, the advice of the sages has fallen on deaf ears. Then again, they didn't have a 5.5-inch LED-backlit widescreen next-generation Retina HD multi-touch display seduction tool offering up so many delicious distractions! So what's the solution? Simple enough, really.

It was Nobel Laureate economist, social scientist, psychologist and decision-making theorist Herbert A. Simon who coined the term 'satisficing' back in 1956 – a nifty portmanteau of the words 'satisfy' and 'suffice'. Simon maintains that we should embrace 'good enough' over 'best' in matters of judgement. Why? Because it's not humanly possible to access every single piece of the information at our disposal, let alone expect our poor brains to process it properly. In other words, there's no such thing as the optimal choice, so why waste precious time looking for something that doesn't exist? Why not embrace a happy medium?

In *The Paradox of Choice*, Schwartz suggests that when making decisions, we fall into one of two categories: satisficers or maximisers. Satisficers tend to focus on achievable goals and thus limit their choices in order to meet personally satisfying criteria. Maximisers, on the other hand, tend to focus on the optimal outcome and thus explore more options than their satisficing counterparts. Such is their exhaustive approach to choice that they ironically are never satisfied. In fact, maximisers are almost always prone to a nasty dose of regret flu as the results rarely live up to their unrealistic expectations.

Furthermore, this self-styled decision bloat isn't restricted to decision-making alone; rather, it tends to spill over into other aspects of our lives. Maximisers possess less effective coping and recovery skills in the face of negative events; are more prone to ruminating over the past; and are strongly affected by what the Joneses are up to. Satisficers are better able to stave off the spectre of remorse by keeping an eye on the present, unfazed by a better possible alternative when they've got something pretty darn good right in front of them. Buddha would've been proud. Schwartz's bottom line? Satisficing is what maximises our happiness.

The bad news? Unless you're Yoda or the Dalai Lama, none of us is truly a dyed-in-the-wool satisficer. In fact, maximising underpins much of our decision-making. The good news? By figuring out how we deal with choice, we can determine what part of our lives needs more balance. And that's what we're about to do. Below are eight satisfaction types, each with their own decision-making traits, to help you identify and understand how you deal with choice, and thus how you can start the search for your happy medium. Brace yourselves, as this knowledge will come in very handy throughout the course of the book. Want in? Then prepare to meet your decision maker.

The Satisfaction Types

A happy man is too satisfied with the present to dwell too much on the future.

ALBERT EINSTEIN, 'MES PROJETS D'AVENIR'

The Maximisers

Frequent Trader is always on the make. Speculative by nature, she treats barter like banter – light and breezy with low commitment and even lower risk of disappointment. From hotel reservations to flight deals, even her mortgage rate, nothing is fixed; everything is flexible and always subject to her own T&Cs.

If she wants out, she trades off, mitigating risk rather than completely cutting her losses, weighing early dinner for two against late-night shopping for one, a mid-week break against a weekend blowout, and her favourite – sneaking off to the pub when a party gets dull. It's not like she's doing the dirty and double-booking – she's just got one eye on the exit sign at all times.

Admittedly, her *Deal or No Deal* approach to the small things in life gives her a sense of control in an otherwise chaotic world. Swapsies don't come cheap, though. There's always a consequence – namely, the regret tax she pays when her plans backfire and she misses last orders. Applied to more valuable life assets, the cost is even higher. Ouch! Those losses smart twice as much as gains.

To be fair, her fast and loose approach to personal satisfaction might stand her in good stead if she focused on her own dividends rather than pining over lost potential. Sadly, there's no trade index for what might have been.

Eternal Bachelor likes to keep his options open – wide open – with one exception: second best. It's simply *never* on the table. Multi-tab browsing consumes his attention to the point of distraction: Spotify-surfing while on Soundcloud, Snapchatting while scrolling through Tinder and Plenty of Fish – even if no one is biting. It's no wonder his connection speed is so slow. By increasing his opportunities, he limits the FOMO (fear of missing out) – or so he thinks. Why get what he wants when he can get what he didn't even know he wanted? Makes sense, no?

Pity life doesn't work that way. His fixation with the future means the present gets summarily shafted. Hence his refusal to buy into the daily grind (he's a laptop entrepreneur, don't you know?) and why the idea of spending a Friday night alone fills him with existential dread. 'Netflix and chill'? More like 'Netflix and cold sweats'.

Sometimes (correction: often), he fantasises about living like an Arabian billionaire prince. It's not as if he's asking for a diamond-encrusted Lamborghini. A Porsche Carrera, on the other hand, would do nicely, as would a Victoria's Secret model girlfriend and the possibility of playing poker with Leo DiCaprio on a Saturday night. His insatiable quest for perfection and his ludicrous expectations means he is not likely to settle or settle down. Likely to be disappointed? Oh, yeah.

Something Better is an alpha status hunter. Peerless in her pursuit of material goods, she spends her most of conscious attention on tracking fair game. Her smartphone constantly calibrates, crowdsources and cross-references the future perfect with ratings, reviews and 'what's hot' listings. The moment she spots an enviable toy, her brain fires with happy hormones and it's open season, folks! Once she has acquired, hashtagged (#thegoodlife) and Instagrammed the object of her affections, the thrill of the chase invariably begins to wane. After a week, she's become used to that walk-in closet/Fendi 'Peekaboo' bag/ La Cornue custom kitchen (delete as appropriate) and before you know it, she's itching for a new trophy that will offer her the same bragging rights.

Obsessed with the staying ahead of the pack, she needs to have the next best thing, until she adapts to that and needs the next best thing and the next and the next – which explains why she's on husband No. 3. Always wanting more, her fixation with status means she's stuck on a treadmill, moving forward but getting nowhere, with contentment always out of reach. It's a zero-sum game, which she loses every time. Just try telling her that.

Wheel Spinner lives in a cognitive cul-de-sac. He doesn't dig decisions. If he makes a choice and regrets it, what then? His game-plan is to wait it out until things are decided for him. Granted, it's a dicey proposition, but he's not exactly action-man material. Everyone knows that.

His attraction to traction means there's little torque in his life, which would explain why he hasn't been promoted – ever. Any time he revs up, he chokes under the pressure and assumes the neutral position. When his life coach does ask about his career goals, he oils up those wheels and pretends he's got things in motion. 'I'm considering my options', 'I'm testing the waters', 'I'm checking the lie of the land', you'll hear him say, all the while giving the impression he's actively tuning something under the hood

So he waits, preferring not to act, just spinning the wheels rather than having his expectations dashed. If he could predict what's up ahead of him, he'd feel less stress, but his reliance on logic means his intuition rarely gets an opportunity to take the wheel. All this wasted effort does is wear out his ability to make satisfying choices.

Even when he does go out on a limb and plays the 'Man with a Plan' card, insecurity makes an ill-timed cameo. Should he have taken a left turn? Might he have saved time turning right? What would have happened had he gone straight ahead? The result? He totally misses out on the present.

Neighbourhood Watch is always looking over her shoulder – or someone else's shoulder for that matter. Ever vigilant, her MO is to be on constant patrol for suspicious status-raising activity. Nothing escapes her watch. Nada. Postal deliveries, trolley-scanning at the supermarket – even innocent handymen get a grilling (oh, the stories they can tell!).

Ironically, it's she who's responsible for the most anti-social behaviour. Between her Facebook, Twitter and Pinterest feeds, her field of social comparison is always becoming bigger, as is her competitive streak. How will she keep up? She's already remortgaged the house. Sell a kidney on eBay?

Her usual game-plan? Call Mary first and find out what she bought. Then finesse her for some info on what Ann and Breda bought too. Call Breda to find out what she *actually* bought (she doesn't trust Mary), then call Ann to corroborate what Mary bought. Then go to town and gazump the lot of them. *Pah!*

Envious and endlessly ruminating, she knows if she looks up, she'll get down so she looks down at others instead. This would explain her reality-TV addiction. It doesn't serve her but does any guilty pleasure? Besides, she can always rely on *Teen*

Mom to make her feel more like a Kardashian. Of course, the path of least resistance would be to approach life with fewer competitive expectations, but what would the neighbours say?

Mystic Meg is fond of forecasting – not that she ever gets it right, mind you. Her ability to predict what's best for her is perpetually bested by her obsession with possibilities. Before she makes any decision, she ensures all future bases are covered. That means consulting her horoscope (daily, weekly and monthly), her tarotscope, her runescope, her angel messages and her daily empath reading from a cross-section of her trusted YouTube gurus.

Then there's her womb reader, her shaman, her numerologist, her Reiki master, her crystal healer, her spirit animal, her feng shui consultant – and let's not forget her aura cleanser, Chakra Khan. She's even tried the cosmic ordering service, but her deliveries never seemed to arrive. Apparently, she's too attached to the outcome.

Incapable of filtering the flotsam of advice, she cherry-picks, scans, skims and distils everything into one broad brushstroke: *think before you act this week. The Scorpio full moon makes things intense!* This predilection for predictions never fails to produce a rogue result. Ironically, had she listened to her own intuition, the answer would've been crystal ball-clear.

List Maker is the ultimate multitasker. Scheduling, organising and kicking life's ass are what tick her box. And you know what that means? Spreadsheets, project maps, clipboards, action points, highlighters and pens designed to make each 'to do' done and done.

The delicious rush that accompanies each successfully archived email and ticked task makes her feel like a professional life-hacker. Who doesn't love bashing a bullet point with a big red 'X'? Some would say her dedication to record-keeping tends to overshadow what's important. These are the same people who made that amateur, Santa, into some sort of productivity guru. Makes a list and only checks it twice? Get off the stage, old man!

She likes to think of herself as uber-productive but when it comes down to it, she's a secret procrastinator. Overwhelmed by the prospect of having to do it all and all to do, she winds up overcommitting and timetabling the impossible. She could choose to do less but she's already got so much on her plate. Another choice would just kill her.

The Satisficers

Grand Grand Grand dines out on appreciation. Not a lot gets her down. Why? Because she's decided that satisfaction is a choice. When it comes to making her mind up, she'll factor in what she needs to know from a menu of options and is prepared to settle for something really good as opposed to waiting for the remote possibility of something better. It's not that she doesn't have standards. She's just realistic and knows when to cut her losses.

Life isn't *always* going to be dipped in awesome sauce. Sometimes you'll get a smattering of pretty delicious or an amuse-bouche of not too bad. Either way, you're still getting fed. Besides, trying too hard to make the universe fit a cookie-cutter version of reality never fails to disappoint, so what's the point in overthinking things? All she can do is her best. After that, there's not a lot else but to leave well enough alone. If life throws her lemons, she soothes herself with an attitude of gratitude and makes a nice vodka and tonic.

MAXIMISERS	SATISFICERS
A maximiser decides rationally.	A satisficer decides intuitively.
A maximiser uses upwards social comparisons.	A satisficer uses self-guidance.
A maximiser works around a problem.	A satisficer goes with the flow.
A maximiser sets unattainable goals.	A satisficer sets achievable goals.
A maximiser is more prone to regret.	A satisficer is almost always satisfied.

Have you determined your satisfaction profile? Still on the fence? Checking your neighbour's answers first? Let me help you out. The cheatsheet on the next page decodes the who, what, how and why of the satisfaction types according to their maximising and satisficing styles. You've probably noticed there's only one satisficer in the bunch. If enough is enough, then one's enough, really.

As you already know, the propensity to maximise underpins many of our decisions, so chances are you're a mix of a few types. It's perfectly normal to be a List Maker in one aspect of your life while playing Frequent Trader in another. Our mission is to figure out how best to improve our satisficing potential so that we can increase our well-being. If you happen to be friendly with Grand Grand Grand, you might pop over for a cuppa and a chat. She's got the goods on this one. In the meantime, let's get a move on. We've got some work to do.

Maximisers and Satisficers at a Glance

WHO?	WHAT?	HOW?	WHY?	MAXIMISER OR SATISFICER?
Frequent Trader	Speculative Non-committal Fears regret	Mitigates opportunity loss by never settling on one choice.	Trades make her feel in control of her decisions amid limitless choice.	Maximiser
Eternal Bachelor	Competitive Narcissistic Perfectionist	Motivated by social comparison. Prone to high expectations and better-than-average self-belief.	Keeps his options open to limit FOMO and maximise his satisfaction levels.	Maximiser

WHO?	WHAT?	HOW?	WHY?	MAXIMISER OR SATISFICER?
Something Better	Competitive Materialistic Obsessive	Motivated by social comparison. Focused on staying ahead of the pack.	Status and material success give her bragging rights and validate her ego.	Maximiser
Wheel Spinner	Avoidant Non-committal Fears regret	Mitigates opportunity loss by choosing not to choose.	Making the choice not to choose makes him feel in control of his decisions.	Maximiser
Neighbourhood Watch	Competitive Envious Insecure	Motivated by social comparison. Ruminates about what others are doing. Tries too hard to keep up.	Social comparison makes her feel more (or less) secure of her status.	Maximiser
Mystic Meg	Speculative Non-committal Fears regret	Mitigates opportunity loss by speculating about the future.	In trying to cover her bases, she doesn't always pick what's best for her.	Maximiser

WHO?	WHAT?	HOW?	WHY?	MAXIMISER OR SATISFICER?
List Maker	Competitive Controlling Insecure	Manages choice by multitasking and hyper-scheduling.	Helps her deal with overwhelm and control the stream of information in her life.	Maximiser
Grand Grand Grand	Secure Present Intuitive	Practices an attitude of gratitude.	Satisfices rather than maximises with decisions.	Satisficer

CHAPTER 2

The Internet, Attention Spans and the Dawn of Distraction

Sorry, What Did You Say?

> No matter what people say about what they value, what matters is
> where they put their attention.
>
> **ARIANNA HUFFINGTON,** *THRIVE*

H ere's a brain tickler for you: what's modern society's rarest commodity? Saffron? 100-year-aged balsamic vinegar? Uranium? Any guesses? Anyone? You're Googling it, aren't you? Oh wait, you left the conversation. Given our attention spans are officially smaller than that of a goldfish (8.25 seconds compared to the 9-second window of our freshwater friends), I guess I should have seen that coming. Maybe I should have prefaced this chapter with a dancing gif, a cat meme (always a crowd-pleaser) or perhaps a 6-second Vine of me mouth-breathing while asleep. Then there's the pressure of a killer headline, a few trending hashtags (#snorecam, #sleepingbeauty) and the vain hope that enough people are amused by my apnoea for it to go viral. Sorry, what was I saying?

And therein lies the rub. Our most precious resource – attention – has become more of a timeshare than a personal asset, yet it is absolutely vital to whether we thrive or simply survive. Images, tweets, snaps, pings, rings, texts, emails, pins and emojis make daily demands on our mental reserves like hungry Tamagotchi pets. The more we feed the beast, the bigger it grows; the bigger it grows, the more it wants; the more it wants, the more distracted and unbalanced we become. It's not just the quantum of our attention that's been hacked; it's the quality too. To paraphrase Paul Donlan, author of *Happiness by Design*, focusing attention on one thing takes it away from another. Focusing attention on several things simultaneously takes it away from them all. (A perfect tweet too – 140 characters!)

Toggling between browser tabs on a conference call while juggling a grande latte and a group chat on Google Hangouts can make us feel like the Grand Poobah of Productivity. It can also make us feel stressed out and anxious, as if we accidentally pressed 'send' and gave our power to that Nigerian prince who needs our help.

This frustrates our decision-making processes, as it is up to us to decide what's worth our consideration and what isn't. Not an easy win, especially for maximisers. Our natural compulsion is to stay alive, to survive by being the proverbial fittest – a hangover from those prehistoric days fending off predators on the Serengeti. Sure, we've come a long way since *Homo erectus* but the primitive itch to spot what's new coming over the horizon is still with us. The future intrinsically has more appeal than the present moment. In caveman terms, it's what separates a death wish from survival.

Granted, it seems spurious to compare checking our smartphones 85 times a day (the average according to a recent study conducted at Nottingham Trent University) with being mauled by an errant wildebeest, but it might go some way to explaining why people lose their will to live when there's no WiFi connection. 404 error – modern man's biggest enemy!

That's the essence of evolution – things change. But one thing that hasn't budged is the brain's love affair with a hunky hormone called dopamine. Known as the 'reward' drug, dopamine is given props for propagating the species by motivating us to seek out food, water, sex and other survival tools. With each success comes a delicious hit of dopamine, followed by a dip. The result? This little beggar is never satisfied, always on the hunt for the unique and the new, always wanting more and more. Translate this to the intravenous novelty drip that is the internet and we've got ourselves one hell of a distraction. The kicker? The hotter and more sustained the pursuit, the sweeter the dopamine high. Addictive? Yes, ma'am. That's the thing about getting hooked: the reward is in the wanting, the thrill of the chase; and when it feeds straight into the palm of your hand, well, that's more than just a diversion. That, my lovelies, is design!

Distraction

Skip this ad in 5 seconds

Start download now

Free download now

Watch later

Actually, watch now

Pop-up

Pop-under

Distractify

BuzzFeed

Click-bait

Click the link

Click the link for more

Click the link NOW for MORE

Click the damn link already!

Boobs

More boobs

Pugs dressed up as cats

Cats dressed up as pugs

Netflix

Netdoctor

Net-a-Porter

21 Borderline Evil Ways to Prank your Flatmate

Autocorrect Fails

What percentage Donald Trump are you?

Everything you need to know about Taylor Swift's Coachella

Here's what Taylor Swift would eat every day if calories didn't count

Watch the latest *Game of Thrones* trailer

Limitless films anytime anywhere just €19.99 per month

Start your subscription today

Start your box-set binge

Constructed reality
(Pre)*Made in Chelsea*
The Real Housewives of Beverly Hills
Rich Kids of Beverly Hills
Rich Kids of Instagram
Rich Kids of the Real Housewives of Beverly Hills on Instagram!
Tonight's jackpot is €12 million. Play now!
Play Candy Crush Saga
Play Farmville
Play Texas Hold 'Em Poker

About cookies on this site
Gluten-free paleo low-carb cookies in just five minutes!
Torch that belly fat fast!
Tired of your job?
Transform your life with this 7-day video series
This is why @kimkardashianwest had to quit breastfeeding
Kardashians
Kardashians
More Kardashians
Lots and lots of Kardashians ...

The Worldwide Web of Distraction

Distracted from distraction by distraction

T.S. ELIOT, 'THE FOUR QUARTETS'

- 39,757 years of our time collectively spent on Facebook every single day
- 5 million images uploaded daily on Instagram
- More than 500 million tweets sent out per day
- 60–80% of people's time on the internet not work-related
- 6 billion hours of YouTube videos viewed each month
- 150 million active daily users on Snapchat

Ah, the internet – sticky, clicky and downright tricky. Its global reach may have bought ease and flow to the way we connect with others, but its combination of novelty and immediate gratification has also created the perfect storm for our mental well-being. Nicholas Carr, author of *The Shallows: What the internet is doing to our brains,* sums it up nicely: 'The net is designed to be an interruption system, a machine geared to dividing attention.' And you know what? He may be right. Lip-sync battles, epic fails, mean tweets and viral video stars have become our favourite snacks at the all-you-can-eat distraction buffet. The more we binge, the more our dopamine starts gurning and doing the happy dance. The more we click, swipe and swoosh, the more foggy and brain-drained we feel, as if deep in a cognitive carb coma.

Surfing the internet is just that: skimming over the waves of information as opposed to plunging deep into its aqueous abyss. Since navigating its information superhighway requires multitasking, it also demands that we shift our attention gears more frequently. The more we steer from topic to topic (like clicking out of a news story to answer an email), the more the brain incurs what scientists call 'switching costs'. In other words, several distractions later, the recovery process placed on the aul noggin can delay engaging your full attention by up to 25 minutes. Think of how many times you pulled the old switcheroo today. Scary, isn't it?

Scarier still is the attendant impact surfing has on our working memory. Quick neuroscience 101: the working memory is the brain's trust account, used to hold items of information before processing and transferring them to long-term learning. The bummer? It's got limited capacity management, which means if it's already full of superfluous stuff, you're not going to squeeze in *War and Peace* too easily. The endless stream of information available to us and our fixation with consuming it (any maximisers out there?) is proven to overload our working memory, which explains why you are sometimes forced to reread what you've read because it didn't quite sink in the first time. Digital dementia isn't just a snazzy shibboleth; it's a growing concern in a world of increasing mental spam. What we gain in speed, we trade off in depth.

And now for another sucker-punch. The more we use the web, the more adept our grey matter becomes at expecting and wanting its fix of brain candy. What's more, it acts like a spoiled toddler and will literally throw its toys out of the proverbial pram if you expect it to read more than 20% of the words on a screen (what the average web user has time to read) when it would much rather be stalking Ryan Gosling on Snapchat (who wouldn't?). It's not that it solely eats up time; it's also secretly snacking on your attention span, your memory and your focus too. The more the mind gets used to fast food, the less it wants to languish over lovingly-prepared meals. In the battle of quality over quantity, the drive-thru wins every time. So, folks, what are we gonna do? The way I see it is, there's only one choice: cold turkey.

Confession Corner

My name is Annmarie and I'm a recovering distraction junkie. I never thought I had a problem until I was faced with a 10-car pile-up on the slippery slope of my own undoing. It's hard to focus when your attention is lying there, fractured in about 10 different places. Not that I noticed.

Here's what happened. I had spent the past few hours at my laptop answering random emails, watching BuzzFeed videos (10 Bad-ass Pets Owning Tumblr!), liking and sharing Facebook posts and poking around Twitter while editing the seventh chapter of *The Happy Closet.* I had more tabs open than a singles bar on a Friday night. And things were about to get interesting. Somewhere in the middle of that mental orgy was a straight-laced party crasher telling me to put on my clothes before I made a *big* mistake. Too late. My attention wasn't merely fractured; it had been splintered into little glass shards, one of which was about to cut me to the quick. Having proofed and fine-tuned my copy, I saved what I thought was Chapter 7 into my 'Final_ Edits' folder:

The file Chapter7.doc already exists. Do you want to replace it?

Before I could even consider that dangerously loaded question, my trigger finger pressed 'Yes.' Instead of saving Chapter 7, I overwrote it with an open document (remember that bar tab?). And there you have it. An entire week's worth killed off in one intoxicated swoop. Cue intense next-level panic. My adrenaline levels were all dressed up with nowhere to go, just swishing around my body in their floor-skimming taffeta skirts grasping at their powdered wigs shouting, 'It's a travesty! A travesty, I say!' (hormones can be prone to the dramatic). I called tech support – a.k.a. my friend Andy – who confirmed what I knew to be true. This one was on me. There was no going back. I had to find an earlier, grossly unedited, version of the chapter and start all ... over ... again. The moral of the story? Instead of using the tool to tell my story, the tool had *become* the story, with muggins the biggest tool of them all.

I know I'm not alone on this one. All it takes is a small brain fault to blow a fuse and trip the whole switchboard. Luckily, all it takes is a simple exercise to raise our awareness so that we don't cause ourselves any further attentional switching costs. Simple is a relative word, but we'll get to that in a moment. In the meantime, brace yourselves and get ready to pull the plug. I'm about to stage an attention intervention!

The Digital Detox

The 'content' of a medium is like the juicy piece of meat carried by the burglar to distract the watchdog of the mind.

MARSHALL MCLUHAN, *UNDERSTANDING MEDIA*

Mindless entertainment is a guilty pleasure – but when it creates a mental muffin top, then it's time to cut back on the cognitive calories. A low-tech fast may appear gimmicky until you take a look at your browser history. Do I hear a whistle blowing? That's the irony about gadgets: they know all of our juicy search secrets ('why does my husband wear panties?', 'Is it illegal to dress up as Santa Claus in New Zealand?'), but they also facilitate our fetishes. It's no wonder we can't think straight. Our hyper-connectivity is what has us permanently poised in a runner's lunge, ready to dash at the first incoming notification. Still think you're immune to the temptation? Let's play a little game.

- Have you ever suffered from 'ringxiety' – the overwhelming urge to check your smartphone regardless of where you are and whether it is even ringing?
- Have you ever felt a buzzing sensation in your pocket only to discover it was a fauxcellarm?
- Have you ever experienced phantom limb – that strange

sensation when you forget your phone and feel like something is missing?

- Have you ever walked into a lamppost/bollard/another person/oncoming traffic (delete as appropriate) while texting, browsing or snapping?
- Have you ever tried to swipe or scroll through menus, magazines or books? Are you trying to scroll through this book right now? You are, aren't you? (Ebook readers excluded, naturally.)

If you've answered yes to even one of these questions, then you, my friend, might be suffering from nomophobia (the fear of being out of mobile phone contact). My advice? Consider giving this digital detox a try.

The aim of this process is to kickstart your mental metabolism. By releasing the pesky toxins (brain fog, forgetfulness, distraction) that build up over time from repeated gadget use, you'll not only increase your attention span but improve its quality and direction too. What's more, you'll begin to regain that crucial online–offline balance – the Holy Grail we'd all follow, if we weren't already following it on Instagram.

Here's the drill. There are two options: the master cleanse and the mini cleanse. In an ideal world, you'd supersize it with a two-week master and top up on a regular basis with the mini cleanse to reap the sustained benefits of a tech time-out. In that ideal world, I'd also be lounging on a beach in Bali asking

Michael Fassbender to apply more sunscreen to my back.

A few things to bear in mind: as with any withdrawal regime, the initial elimination phase can be a humdinger. Expect what's commonly referred to as a 'healing crisis'. In other words, prepare to feel cranky, fidgety and/or fit to be tied. These feelings, although anti-social, are key to understanding how you've been allocating your attention. The stronger the sense of unease, the more you'll benefit from easing offline, so put on your big-girl pants and tough it out. What's more, the process itself is temporary so as these emotions pass, what remains will be a greater sense of clarity and purpose. And remember, those big-girl pants have special powers. Don't underestimate them.

A small caveat: don't embark on this detox if you are currently dieting, planning a wedding, playing host to long-lost relatives or doing anything that requires a full-frontal display of your mental and emotional faculties. The phrase 'balls to the wall' comes to mind. The second you hit a speed wobble, your willpower levels will clap out and you'll be trolling celebrity gossip sites in a moment of weakness.

Likewise, if you work in an industry that requires regular online usage (hello, social media mavens!), travel a lot or are expected to be on call, be realistic and opt for the mini cleanse – a mere 48 hours of your time. Unless, of course, you've planned a week's getaway, which would be the perfect opportunity to disconnect. FullContact, a high-tech firm in Denver, pays their staff $7,500 to go on holiday and totally unplug – that means the week-long abstinence course – promising not to check work emails, texts or calls. Not that I'll be coughing up that type of coin, but we're in it for the satisfaction, not the money. Right? Glad we cleared that up.

Finally, let me clarify one more thing. As drastic as a blanket ban may seem, there's a method to my madness. Those who've read *The Happy Closet* will know me as a stickler for habits. In fact, I dedicated an entire book to how they shape our happiness. Here's a recap. Warning: spoiler alert!

Habits are formed and stored in a part of the brain called the basal ganglia, which dates back to our cave-people days. This prehistoric PA keeps the cognitive cogs in motion by making habits 'automatic' once they've been mastered. She then files them away under 'unconscious', allowing the conscious mind to get on with being the big boss. So effective is the basal ganglia at office admin, she keeps track of everything – for life. In other words, habits never disappear. Ever. Which means those sneaky hours updating your Pinterest boards are on your permanent record. The good news? The brain can't distinguish between a good and a bad habit, which means it holds your peerless PowerPoint skills in equal esteem. Score! Over time and with repetition, habits happen without our permission and often with little persuasion. The bad news? These habits become so unconscious that it only takes the smallest trigger to access them from our memory, the smallest distraction to catch us on the hop and – BAM! You've accidentally sent your boss a pin of a pug doing yoga (#downwarddog).

Remember when your mother would take away a toy so you could 'think about what you've done?' Well, the principle of the digital detox is more or less the same. Mothers are smart like that. By disrupting the reward cycle that is holding your attention captive to the internet, your conscious mind is given more space to consider the ramifications of its less salubrious habits. The truth is, unless you work for FullContact and have a dangling carrot of $7.5k to keep you away from the naughty step, you'll probably have access to regular temptation like workplace internet access or gadgets belonging to friends and family. This detox really does rely on you to do the graft, which is why you have to want to do it and why you have to have a juicy reward at the end of the process to make this worthwhile. It's a tough one, but if you're serious about creating balance and finding that middle ground for yourself, it all starts here. Okey dokey. Let's make like a fast and get this cleanse moving.

The Master Cleanse: Abstinence

Objective:

- To put the kibosh on multitasking and create more conscious internet usage patterns.
- To eliminate distractions and increase attention spans.

Best for: Heavy or habitual users

Timeframe: One week

You'll need:

- A notebook and a pen to record the experience (keep these handy as you'll be using them throughout this book).
- To remove every app from every device (including email – unless it's essential to your work). This means putting headphones on ice too.
- To install a site-blocking extension on your laptop/desktop browser for a seven-day period.
- A task team to keep you accountable. In other words, tell everyone you know. There's nothing people like more than to play bad cop, given half a chance and a bag of peanut M&Ms.
- A 'competing response' (psychology-speak for an alternative behaviour with personal resonance) to keep you occupied along the way. For example, reading a book, regular walks or embarking on a pet project you've put on pause.
- A reward for successfully completing the process. This will motivate you to focus on the bigger picture. Aim for something super sensory like an aromatherapy massage, killer seats at a sold-out concert or a slap-up meal at your favourite restaurant.

Process:

- Keep a daily record of the experience in your notebook. Notice how it makes you feel (nervous, irritable, empty, relieved) and how these emotions evolve throughout the week.

- Pay attention to any behaviours pursuant to not achieving your desired reward: minimising, bargaining, gnashing and grinding of teeth, next-level FOMO.
- Keep tabs on any rewards you thought you would miss:
  - Did you survive without checking Facebook every six minutes?
  - How does the new sense of mental space feel: liberating, calming, excruciating?
  - Did it make you more or less anxious not to hear notifications on your phone?
- Jot down the new things you notice, paying attention to the five senses: sight, sound, smell, touch and taste. For example, the smell of coffee, the sounds of the city.
- At the end of the week, replace the removed apps and disable any site-blocking extensions. Honourably discharge your family and friends.
- Keep your notebook for another week but skip journaling for the first five days. Allow your conscious mind to regain its usual focus and routine before checking in on Day 6. When you do, pay attention to the following:
  - How do you feel now? Are you calmer? Is decision-making easier or more difficult? Were you forced to satisfice more or rely on your intuition without having a search engine at hand?

- Has your usage changed? Did you decide to evict any pointless apps that were occupying your digital real estate? Have you determined which ones give your life more ease and flow? For me, it's online banking, Uber or Hailo taxi booking services, Google Maps (I have zero sense of direction) and MindBody (a wellness app that allows me to book into local yoga or gym classes around the country). Everything else is negotiable.
- Are you more conscious of when, where and why you reach for your phone or tablet, multitask or mindlessly browse?
- Did you find an opportunity for doing and noticing other things or was it just a drag?
- Did you rely more on your competing response to help you? How did it feel to realise the potential in something you'd neglected?
- Did you quit the cleanse? If so, why? Was the habit too ingrained or was the social anxiety just too much?

The Mini Cleanse: The 48-Hour Fast

Objective:

- To be used as maintenance after completing a master cleanse.

- To be used independently to clear out the mental cobwebs and regain attentional focus.

Best for: Functional and casual users; the time-strapped in need of a brain boost

Timeframe: 48 consecutive hours

Process:

- Follow the Master Cleanse process on page 37 on two consecutive days of your choice.
- So how did it go? Are you feeling refreshed or are you rocking gently in a foetal position mumbling something about the Kardashians? As your dopamine see-saw levels off, your mind should feel decluttered and more receptive to what's around you.

Allowing for time offline lets us upgrade our attention with intention – applied mindfulness in action. It also creates space for reconnecting with those pursuits that add layers to our day-to-day existence. By becoming more conscious of what you expect from your time, you're better positioned to make more deliberately satisfying choices and approach your happy medium. You're also less inclined to be riddled with remorse at losing valuable hours FaceStalking old flames and school friends. The problem is you cannot access this sweet spot of satisfaction if your mind is distracted. You will simply wind up doing several things to 'meh' level instead of one thing well. Or, in my case, being publicly shamed by my peers. That got your attention, didn't it? Ah, go on. I'll spill the beans.

Confession Corner

I was on vacation with friends in a quaint whitewashed Italian village. The villa balcony overlooked a Mediterranean promise of verdant virgin trails and blue vistas. It couldn't have been more perfect. It was our last evening before we had to return the Life of Reilly to its rightful owner and head home. Most of us went to bed. I made the excuse that I was staying up to watch a documentary about the House of Valentino on the telly. This was in part true. I lasted about, oh, two minutes before I clicked on a seemingly innocent hyperlink to reality show *The Only Way Is Essex* while browsing on my tablet. Attention, how are ya? I was Brentwood-bound and there was little I could do to stop it. Fake tans, hair extensions, vajazzles, oh my! Not to mention them diamond geezers, innit.

To be fair, this wasn't my first time at the rodeo. I have long been a secret reality-TV binger, regularly mainlining flimsy plot lines and fake relationships like a hardened brain food junkie. I may have prided myself on a clutter-free wardrobe, but my brain was a hoarder's paradise. I could no longer issue a running sentence of Italian (despite having previously been fluent), but I could tell you which members of the *Jersey Shore* house were *actually* Italian. I couldn't remember the names of the couple in the adjacent villa but I could name the three finalists on the first season of *America's Next Top Model*. I couldn't remember what I had for breakfast but I knew that I could catch up with *Hell's Kitchen* on YouTube once I finished my Estuary escape. Or so I thought. Hovering over the sofa was one of my travel pals who witnessed the entire episode. I've never lived it down. Masquerading as a cultured Italophile; slumming it as a docu-soap doyenne. My weak protestations weren't gonna fly. It was obvious my actions and intentions were sleeping in separate beds. And to whom did distraction pay her after-hours call? You guessed it – muggins.

After the mass ridicule had subsided, *three years later,* I began to notice just how slapdash I was with my attention. I took it for completely for granted until it packed up and bailed out, leaving my sorry ass with a head full of useless tat that I couldn't sell on eBay if I tried. As mentioned earlier, attention focused on one thing means attention taken away from another. Remember our efficient PA, the basal ganglia? Well, she may archive habit files but over time, if they're not used, the brain makes an executive decision to cut them loose. So that's what happened to those four years learning to play the clarinet! What's more, if a certain habit is developed and starts flexing some muscle, it will crowd out its weaker competitors. See: reality TV versus real life.

The good news? With some balance, we can learn to displace distraction, increase the quality of our attention and, in turn, make more satisfying choices and achieve a happy balance in the present. It's up to us, though, to decide what's worth paying attention to. Luckily, we've got some satisfying food for thought in the next chapter. In the meantime, why not fill up on some of these happiness hacks for the road?

Happiness Hacks

BEWARE THE BLIND SPOT

Check you out! You walking, talking, texting, snapping, swooshing hot thang! Aren't you just a dollop of fabulous with a cherry on top? Well, that's what the dishy barista who dishes out your flat white every morning thinks. Shame you haven't been paying attention. Psychologists call it 'inattentional blindness' – the inability to notice and register new things while distracted. Some call it the reason you're still single. Might that be because your most intimate relationship is with an inanimate object? Some friendly advice: get present and stop missing what's right in front of your eyes.

Good for: Frequent Trader, Eternal Bachelor, List Maker

GET ENGAGED

There's a hot phone in your hand, a fog over your brain and a name on the tip of your fuzzy tongue. This isn't a new drinking game; it's an attentional hangover. If heavy internet use has you in a perpetual mind-funk, it's time for an old-fashioned cure. Stretch that atrophied attention span by playing with your brain's natural elasticity. Engage in time-expanding offline activities that require your full focus and total physical engagement. The best bit? What you do is totally your call. Baking, knitting, gardening, sudoku, reading, hiking, origami – anything that marshals your attention to the task at both hands (have you ever seen anyone attempting a single crochet bind-off and texting at the same time? Thought so.). Then repeat, repeat, repeat until it begins to crowd out the silly distractions that you thought to be oh-so-important.

Good for: All types

LOVE YOUR LIMITS

Limits are like credit controllers. We know it's 'their job', but it doesn't stop us disliking them. That said, a little reframing is all that's necessary to take our limits from buzzkill bureaucrats to mindful time managers. This is especially pertinent when creating an offline–online balance. For example, when writing, I put my phone is on airplane mode and I allocate set times in the morning and evening to reply to emails and update social media. Between those times, the StayFocusd extension blocks out distraction sites online and my Gmail account is set to Out of Office. This practice is also commonly referred to as 'the notions destroyer' – just in case I had any.

Good for: Frequent Trader, Eternal Bachelor, Wheel Spinner

PLAN IT, DAMMIT

Setting times for internet usage is like setting the table for dinner. It creates space for it to become a ritual rather than a routine. Likewise, contextualising our data meals with a beginning and an end sends a message to the brain that it is full. There's a parallel between eating food and eating data: in both instances, the brain is sent a message that it feels full if we sit down and create a conscious 'meal time'. The most purposeful way to use the internet is in creating time-slots for usage. Those who consume information as a method for distraction or while on the run are more likely to fall foul of always feeling hungry despite being overfed with information. Granted, the Google oracle is great in an emergency, but not everything requires a fast answer.

Good for: All types

FIND FAULT IN THE DEFAULT

When we plug ourselves into too many devices at once, we're bound to blow a fuse. And when we do, the only thing to do is switch off the circuit board before resetting the trips. This process allows you to figure out what's interfering the most with your connection or whether you've short-circuited yourself into oblivion.

Test your daily routine for potential faults. Do you answer emails on your tablet before you get out of bed? Use your phone as an alarm clock? Perhaps you use work on your laptop while watching TV? Then use this opportunity to test out more purposeful patterns like enforcing a tech embargo at meal times and when you have company over or implementing #TechFreeTuesday. By creating more deliberate usage habits, your patterns of unconscious swiping and scrolling will begin to wane, your craving for novelty will begin to subside and a happy balance will fill the distraction vacuum.

Good for: All types

JUST SAY 'NO'

Multitasking makes you stupid. Fact. Scientific studies have proven that this ironically unproductive behaviour decreases levels of grey matter in the brain. The new black? Downgrading from multi to mono. Before allowing your ego to take the wheel to do fancy handbrake turns, why not take the keys out of the ignition until that boy racer in your head gets bored and slings his hook? Try committing to completing one task, whether that's reading a book or booking a flight, without compromising valuable attention attending to beeps, blips, snaps and other audible intrusions. Need inspiration? Think of my 'Save As' confession and think again.

Good for: Frequent Trader, List Maker

REWIRE YOUR REWARDS

You know what I love best about the brain? It's as gullible as a con man in love. Despite its formidable reputation, it can be convinced of just about anything. According to Kelly McGonigal, lecturer at Stanford University and author of *The Willpower Instinct: How Self-Control Works*, the brain can learn to rewire its reward expectations with the right coaching. That means keeping some feel-good goodies on standby, as recommended in the digital detox. Each time you rumble your hand having a sneaky fumble in your handbag, just tell your brain to hold off a little longer as you've got a much more satisfying reward in store – and be sure that you do. Your brain may be gullible, but it's not stupid.

Good for: All types

MOST WANTED

Florida State University researchers have discovered that mobile phone notifications alone can distract us from attention-demanding tasks, even when we choose to ignore them. The culprit? Dopamine. This frisky hormone gets its reward not just in the checking of our devices but the pure wanting of it. Do you need to be notified about the 200 or so emails that land in your inbox each day as they arrive? Didn't think so. Now turn off those notifications and stop your mind from wandering. You'll be happier for it.

Good for: All types

STOP, LOOK, LISTEN!

Imagine the scenario. You're having some banter with a pal who breaks the momentum to check her phone. You get back into your gossip groove and she does it again – and again, and again. Annoying, much? Very much. You can't control being 'phubbed' (phone-snubbed) by others but you can lead by example. Paying attention is the ultimate compliment, whether it's making eye contact or listening intently to what someone is saying. Both are forms of presence and can be especially powerful mindfulness tools. The next chat you have, listen and respond in a way that shows you haven't mentally checked out. Pay attention to the eye colour, shape, even the lash length of the person you are speaking to. Bring this awareness to your interactions and notice the difference. Just don't do the stalker stare.

Good for: All types

NEED TO KNOW BASIS

Did you know it's impossible to block Mark Zuckerberg on Facebook and that eight feet is the ideal height from which to drop buttered toast should you wish it to land right side up? Wait, there's more where that came from. In fact, there's always more where that came from. Googling random facts can satisfy our curiosity, but it also kills our sense of wonder and, as we discovered earlier in this chapter, can compromise our working memory, attention span and focus too. We all love to snack on trivia titbits but try limiting the cognitive candy lest your brain keeps asking for more. Now, where's my toast?

Good for: Mystic Meg, List Maker

CHAPTER 3

Anti-Social Networking

Left to Our Own Devices

The generation that had information, but no context. Butter, but no bread. Craving, but no longing.

MEG WOLITZER, *THE UNCOUPLING*

icture this. There's a tanned girl in a bikini holding an extra-whip frappuccino and an ultrasound scan. Her fingers are fanned to display a new leopard print gel manicure and ... OMG ... one hell of a sparkler! Is Starbucks officiating shotgun weddings at the beach? Not quite. Keep reading. Next to her is a dude with his top off, flexing a tattooed arm. He looks ripped. Don't piss him off. Beside the brooding gymbo is a disgruntled cat dressed like the Easter Bunny. Around his neck is a sign that reads 'Hopping Mad!' Ah, the LOLs! And wait, two perfect children just arrived dressed head-to-toe in #babyGap, holding a tray of gluten-free, sugar-free, dairy-free vegan cupcakes. They've been told if they fake-smile long enough for Mommy to get the shot, they can have one each. OK, the whole damn tray. Just stop wiggling!

Sounds familiar? Of course it does. The online landscape is populated with endless images of humble-brags, ego-stroking and next-level narcissism. This composite of clichés may well be ironic but we're all part of the same picture. In fact, we've helped to create it. 'But I've detoxed my digital life,' I hear you say. True. And thus you are better prepared to swallow this spoon of truth serum doing the airplane your way. Open wide!

We're all guilty. Guilty as charged. We should know better than to participate in competitive posting but we can't seem to help ourselves. Why? It's not as if we're archiving Hallmark moments on the regular. Most of our day-to-day dealings are unassuming, gently humming away in the background – not canvassing for a thumbs-up emoji. That said, a quick scan of the internet makes it seem like the entire world is celebrating something, and this has a curious way of sucker-punching our self-esteem. Logic assures us it's the green-grass filter at play. After all, not everyone could be #lovinglife in the Maldives (could they?) but that doesn't stop the green-eyed monster from hijacking our common sense and photobombing our sense of satisfaction.

The majority of us are wise to the ever-changing algorithms used by social networks and search engines to capture our shrinking attention spans, to predict what we are most likely to click or, in marketing speak, to get us to 'engage' with content that is 'meaningful'. These digital divinators aren't exactly going to deliver us posts about someone who almost made the big time but took a job selling insurance instead; they're certainly not going to serve you up a pic of a half-eaten piece of toast when there's a champagne toast to be had; and they definitely won't recommend a 10-year-old Volkswagen Golf when your retinal satisfaction could be better served by a brand new Range Rover Sport. This selection bias makes us think of the best as being normal, which can cause us to confuse reality with what exists online. It's life alright, just somebody else's – but try telling your inner maximiser that.

Call it cyber-Darwinism, a latent hominid hangover or survival of the famous, but part of our fascination with maintaining a social media 'presence' boils down to the need to be seen – and to control the impression we're all so keen to make. Look at me on holidays in India! Look at my bee-pollen smoothie! Look at my rose gold Apple MacBook which matches my Gianvito Rossi crystal sandals and Charlotte Tilbury bronzer, which happens to be displayed on my sheepskin rug. I spent three hours preparing this flat shoot – look at it, dammit! The big scam? Keeping our head above WiFi-enabled waters isn't a one-shot deal. Creating new online personas may look tempting but reinvention has its price. Although social media allows us the luxury of making a first impression twice, it also demands that we repeat the process over and over again. Want to get noticed online? The measure of success is impressions – *plural.*

The next time you scroll through a news feed, think about where you stop and linger the most. Then have a quiet word with your brain, which is playing bouncer to the queue of information looking to get past your velvet ropes. Due to its limited capacity, it's under strict instructions to only allow the remarkable – the VIP of communications, that superlative 1% – to make a conscious impact on our mental establishment, which could explain our itch to update and enhance the version we present of our lives online, the self we want to be seen to be. I'm looking at you, Something Better!

And so it goes. We compete on someone else's terms. We make decisions that aren't compatible with our long-term satisfaction. We compare and oh, do we despair. The way I see it we've got two choices: continue keeping up with the Joneses or call time on the tomfoolery. All the self-awareness in the mind, body, spirit aisle will do you sod-all good unless you put some muscle to your hustle. So chaps, let's get moving. First, I've got (another) confession to make ...

Confession Corner

'Put the phone down. Step away from the phone now.' I really should've listened the first time Neil warned me. I could've got off lightly – a rookie misdemeanour, a first-time offence but things had gone too far. I was out of control.

What started as a few innocent social media posts about our holiday ended up as a full-blown FaceBragging rampage. In my defence, I got a tad swept away by it all. It was my first time in Thailand and, by jingo, everyone was going to know about it. My blatant boasts were indeed criminal. I was guilty of every conceivable social media cliché, including but not limited to: hot-dog legs on the beach, drinking a beer on the beach, sandy feet selfies on the beach, lighting paper lanterns on the beach, eating fresh lychees from a banana leaf on the beach, impromptu picnics on the beach. Did I mention we were on a beach – a coral beach, in March?

It may have been paradise in Koh Tao but trouble was on the horizon when I continued to ignore my friend's sage advice. As I was screengrabbing the morning weather forecast (30 degrees and rising!), Neil caught me in the act. 'Annmarie, stop!' He pointed to the news feed on his phone. And with that, the sh*tstorm descended. There it was. Snow. Lots of it. Feet of it. The evidence was irrefutable.

Ireland was covered in an Arctic blanket. Mother Nature, it appeared, had to spend a penny and took an unseasonal dump on our otherwise green isle. So as we were topping up our tans, our friends were strapping on snow boots to get to work in one piece.

The lack of 'likes' on the dozens of ill-timed iPhone shots I posted indicated the sheer gravity of my gaffe. A slew of angry-face emojis and comments such as 'Don't come home' made it clear that I may have overstepped the mark. Neil was right. It was time to put the phone down. Not that I had much use for it after that. I didn't just suffer the slings and arrows of outrageous social media misfortune; I also got my first taste of Bangkok Belly, which became my loyal companion for the remainder of the trip. Serves me right for all of the crap I was posting. Naturally, that part of the holiday remains undocumented.

The Internet's Most Wanted

> I should fancy that crime was to them what art is to us, simply a method of procuring extraordinary sensations.
>
> **OSCAR WILDE,** *THE PICTURE OF DORIAN GRAY*

We all stand accused, to a greater or lesser degree, of anti-social media misconduct. The question is: why do we risk social exclusion/looking like a plonker (delete as appropriate) for the apparent reward of broadcasting our life moments? Remember our friend, dopamine? As we know, the reward of posting about ourselves online is in the emotional pay-off – the intoxicating cocktail of validation by likes that gets us all fired up. But as is always the case with dopamine, once is never enough. We want, nay demand, feedback on our self-styled snapshots on a constant loop – even if the shots themselves drive us (and others) to distraction. In our defence, most of the time, we're not even aware we're doing it. That's because, as the digital detox proved (see Chapter 2), many of our online habits are unconscious. Sometimes all it takes an external agent (hello, Neil!) to slap on the mental handcuffs and give us a ruddy good telling off. Often, however, a more considered investigation is what's needed to determine our online behaviour and so capture the attention thieves and dopamine dealers that swindle our satisfaction. More on that shortly. In the meantime, check out the internet's most wanted below and see if you can identify yourself in the line-up.

The Name Dropper is a shrewd operator. Charged with multiple counts of tailgating, this lady's not averse to tagging celebrities to appear more connected. Her MO? An @ symbol and an itchy trigger finger. Oh, and the upper hand. Always. 'Bumped into @saoirse_ronan again at my local coffee spot. And no, I'm not dishing the deets. It's our little secret! LOL!' Breezy, perhaps? But beneath her brio is a lingering insecurity that she's keen to hide lest her cover is blown. Busted for being ordinary? Oh, the shame!

The Influencer deals in self-promotion. A savvy strategist, her brand is her weapon and her Klout Score a source of personal pride. Call her calculating but everyone knows it's a numbers game. That perfectly-lit shot of her staring into the middle distance while holding a latte? Paid for (just check the back links). That candid photo of her eating ice-cream on the beach? Sponsored (she's dairy-free, btw). Capitalising on the currency of trust, she leverages her persuasion to 'help connect clients and customers'. She just doesn't tell you that. This gig is all about being authentic. Trust me: it's not as easy as it looks.

The Image Crafter has a perfect life. At least, that's what she leads you to believe. Some call her a fraud; she likes to think of herself as a lifestyle curator who imparts her vision to her thousands of followers (even if she did buy most of them). Accuse her of inorganically beefing up those audience numbers and she'll swear on her quinoa tofu salad that she's a vegan. Ethics are hugely important to her, which is why she ~~copied~~ referenced Goop's post on paraben-free lube and condoms. She's not *that* self-serving. OK then, she is. But isn't everybody?

The Humble Bragger is ubiquitous, always at large and thus difficult to apprehend. Diffusing her boasts with the #blessed hashtag and a fusillade of false modesty, she gets away with all sorts of shenanigans. Self-deprecation is her signature move, one that allows her to freely showcase her achievements. 'What a morning! First, my two sweet kiddos spoiled me with roses, a beautiful card and a delicious homemade cake. Then my hubby gave me a foot rub while singing me my favourite Adele song. What did I do to deserve this life? I feel so privileged to be a mother and a wife today and every day.' Oh. Dear. God.

The Blatant Boaster has no filter. A digital delinquent, he stands accused of multiple breaches of good conduct and online etiquette. His lack of self-awareness is matched by flagrant displays of swagger: trips to Las Vegas, flash car selfies (do test drives count?), wads of cash, gang signs and gold-plated sneakers. Unlike the Humble Bragger, he never covers his tracks and is more likely to be charged with being a public nuisance, hidden from a news feed or blocked. All this does is add more fuel to the fires of his international playboy fantasy. Haters be hatin'. Yeah, of course, buddy. DELETE.

The Retrospective likes to look back if for no other reason than to show you how good she's had it. Holiday season and major life events are prime time for scheduling epic posts beginning with 'It's been one hell of a year/divorce party/ mid-life crisis/30-day detox' and ending with 'Here's to more memories!' Concealed in the nostalgia? A detailed laundry list of why she's so lucky: achievements, acquisitions, boasts and borrowed names that have 'made me the person I am' – one of the internet's biggest copycat criminals. No comparison there.

The Egosurfer isn't the outdoorsy type. Cresting the manifold mentions of his name in online searches is his preferred sport.

'I'm just checking my digital footprint,' you'll hear him say, until he gets some dirty lickings in a comment thread that he feels it incumbent upon him to personally defend – and then complain about online for the rest of the week. Cue: wipe out. On the days he finds something rad with his name attached, his ego is waxed and ready to rock (look out for the humble-brag). But rue the day he finds nothing. Invisibility? Game over. That's the thing about spectator sports: you can never win.

Spot the Instagram odd ones out

duck faces

ducks making faces

bathroom selfies

bathroom groupies

the red carpet

some brown carpet

front row at a fashion show

front row at mass

five-carat diamond ring

five carrots

walking down the aisle

walking out of divorce court

inspirational quotes

reality checks

wing of a plane

a plain wing

snuggling in bed

hungover in bed

about to board a private jet

about to board EasyJet

blowing kisses

blowing noses

someone flashing a peace sign

someone flashing a stop sign (that I'd like to see)

Crime Scene Investigation

You are what you share.

CHARLES LEADBEATER, *WE-THINK*

Who are you? Who, who, who, who? I really wanna know. Ah, go on. Tell me who you are. Do any of those profiles look familiar? Have you identified with any Shady O'Grady behaviour or are you vehemently protesting your innocence? Look, we're all very quick to point the finger of blame at someone else. Rarely, if ever, do we turn it inwards and see how perhaps we are operating a similar attention-seeking racket. I certainly didn't. And therein lies the rub. To achieve our happy medium, we've got to raise our awareness and confess to our own capers. Don't expect any guided meditations (not just yet). You won't get off that lightly. This calls for a crime scene investigation: an exercise designed to demonstrate how our anti-social media conduct impacts others. Nothing like a naked bulb and hard evidence to shine some light on the truth. Consider owning up as an act of presence. Mindfulness involves being conscious of our actions, which in turn makes adopting a victim mentality a cop-out. Avoid it at all costs. Get set to cue the Horatio Cane sunglasses montage. This investigation is officially underway.

For this exercise, you'll need:

- A smartphone, tablet or laptop
- A notebook and a pen

- An honest friend to play star witness
- Two hats, as you'll be playing both chief investigator and the accused.

Here's how this shakedown goes down. Your job as chief investigator is to collect, preserve and analyse the body of evidence given to you by your witness. This is the part where you put your inner maximiser to good use. So far, we've seen how maximising can interfere with our happiness levels by fostering unrealistic expectations; now let's look at how they can be enhanced. Maximisers are undeniably conscientious, conduct thoroughly exhaustive searches and will dumpster-dive through archives of trash to get their answers. With the help of your witness, it's your gig to collect as many samples of evidence to create a strong case – against yourself, admittedly.

Your witness should be an honest friend with whom you share a reciprocal social media friendship and a real-time bond that'll make handling the truth a lot easier. Consider it the opposite of a two-way mirror: he or she is waiving the right to anonymity, which makes the process more transparent. Understanding how your actions affect others is key to creating your happy medium. The fact that you've got a strong connection with your witness also means you won't be putting a bounty out on his or her head should you be exposed as being a name-dropping, image-crafting humble bragger.

Now that housekeeping is out of the way, our first priority is the crime scene. Pick the social network you both communicate on the most. Make a short list of the posts or stories on your feed or wall that your witness points to as examples of your most blatant anti-social behaviour. Slap on those government-issued rubber gloves and prepare to go deep into your timelines. Dig for the nostril-flaring, gag-reflux-inducing 'Did I really say that?' moments. For each post, jot down the following: prime suspect, crime, weapon, suspected motivation and emotional fall-out for the witness observing the crime.

Next, get your witness (or witnesses) to write out a full impact statement, taking care to include sequential evidence from the visual trigger you posted to their emotional reaction and any ensuing reactions from the post in question. Then examine their collective proof. Give your ego a long lunch break and grab yourself some coffee and humble pie as the testimony is read aloud.

Feeling nervous? Allow me to take the lead. Note: the following deposition was taken from a friend who shall remain nameless.

Prime suspect: My friend Annmarie – a.k.a. the Far-Flung Felon
Crime: The Blatant Boast
Weapon: An endless stream of 'look at me!' photographs in south-east Asia
Suspected motivation: To impress those at home with her exotic holiday

Emotional fall-out for the witness:

- Feelings: Irritation, envy
- Reaction: Carb-loading, mental daggers, scrolling obsessively through her Facebook photo album
- Reason: Snowmaggedon hit Ireland. I had been hugging the radiator and watching my skin turn a curious shade of blue.

Witness Impact Statement: *I clicked the Facebook app on my phone one evening in March. I noticed a post from my friend who was on holidays in Thailand. She was holding a glass of champagne by her beach hut. The caption read: 'Our hideaway for the next few days before island-hopping!' I thought 'Lucky girl' and nothing more of it until the following morning when I woke up to two feet of snow and a cyber assault of holiday updates – one after another after another. I felt totally blindsided, annoyed and envious at the same time. I mentally poked at a voodoo doll of her in my head and Googled cheap holidays in Tenerife before putting on my ski salopettes and a balaclava to leave the house.*

So *that's* who put a curse on my small intestines! All joking (and stomach cramps) aside, hearing a witness account of my brag-a-thon was a short sharp shock to my conscious awareness. Posting a few (hundred) holiday snaps seemed harmless enough at the time, but that's only because I wanted to be seen – on a beach, in March. Can't slap a filter on that fact too easily. Cue: mild mortification.

Looking for a real eye-opener? Do this with as many samples of your own internet infractions that you can handle. What do you see? Is there a thread? Are certain patterns emerging? If so, these are the behavioural deviations that you need to address to maintain a holistic happy medium.

What's worth remembering is that although social networking may trigger symptoms of comparison, we're always the ones holding the weapon. It's up to us to clear up our internal world so that we don't jump the gun. This applies equally to offline connections and situations approached from a place of lack. By shifting our perspective, we can learn to be satisfied with who and where we are in the present moment. Trust me, I'm an inexpert expert on the subject, as the following story illustrates. Prepare to swap your inspector cap for a hat-tip to introspection. This bad boy is one for internal affairs.

Confession Corner

Not too long ago I signed up for a networking event. Fresh from writing my first book, I was jonesing for some face-time, an elbow rub or two with those who might be interested in hearing about my hardback baby. Having never been to one of these name-badged conferences before, I had no real frame of reference bar the odd TEDTalk I had seen on YouTube. So I found a seat, got comfy and listened to the keynoter's opening address about having drive.

Buzzwords like 'the fast lane' and 'full throttle' reeled about like whirling dervishes. Having never sat my driver's test, the irony wasn't lost on me; nor was the memory of asking my instructor why we used gears.

Without warning, the microphone turned to the crowd. 'What motivates you to get out of bed in the morning?' asked the speaker. Given I can barely find my face before 9 am without being hooked intravenously to a French press, the first (and only) word to come to mind was 'coffee.' I was faced with a moment of full-speed panic.

I racked my brains for a killer LinkedIn answer – something inspiring that alluded to my recent book birth. The more I searched for the perfect answer, the more I thought of Tesco's Finest Guatemalan blend. The more I thought of coffee, the more I realised I had to pee. There was no sneaking out to the ladies here, not unless I wanted to be caught rapid.

As the microphone inched nearer, hands rose higher and stories got taller. The bar was officially raised. It said, 'Come and have a go if you think you're hard enough, missus!' Truth was, I wasn't. I felt intimidated and blindsided all at once. Wasn't this a place to connect and inspire? Not compete and defeat. I didn't see anywhere on the invitation where it said 'Bring your A-game, you'll need it.' And the game was definitely on.

It was as if Sheryl Sandberg and Miss Teen America morphed into a type-A hybrid – one eye on the Nikkei index, the other on saving the world. What struck me was that nobody (including me) raised a hand to say, 'I'm not so sure what motivates me', 'I'm in it for the pension' or 'Make mine a strong Americano!'

And then came the coup de grâce – an exercise in one-upmanship that would make Darwin himself blush. 'What motivates me most is giving back to the children of Calcutta,' answered the hand that delivered the final blow. Well, what do you know – Mother Flaming Teresa turned up. A lady with dark hair and a serious suit leaned in toward me and whispered, 'Game over. No one competes with Calcutta.' She was right. Well played. With that I sunk a bit further into my chair and quietly Googled 'sixth gear'.

Competition isn't anything new. Attention-seeking is part of our DNA. It's what helps us, from an evolutionary perspective, to get ahead. That said, our predisposal to self-auditing by measuring ourselves against others can be more of a hindrance than a help. As creatures of social comparison, we continually wonder how happy we are compared to others: upwards and downwards, we look for clues to reinforce our progress, to reassure us that we're moving forward. Often, however, we strive for validation beyond our comfort zone, creating unnecessary stress and anxiety by comparing ourselves with the leaders of the pack.

In my case, it was clear I was playing someone else's game, but I still allowed myself to be swept up in the score-keeping. I may have been proud of my book, but my insecurity was obvious. Why hadn't I started a Reiki practice for sick animals in my spare time? Surely I could have fit in an MBA somewhere in my schedule? The funny thing? The reward for me had always been in writing the book. Yet in a matter of moments, I kicked my happy medium to the curb and spent the next hour or so wondering why I wasn't more.

And to think, all it would have taken was a mini mental pep talk to calm my inner maximiser, who was still in overdrive about the day's crash and burn. This simple key to change? It starts with learning how to tune into our intuition: that knowing voice who's got dibs on our cognitive cruise-control. Got a pen and that notebook handy? Good. It's time to find sixth gear.

Finding the Signal

Comparison is normal, human and expected. In fact, it can be a mighty mindfulness tool, if wielded appropriately. Comparison, like a state-of-the-art GPS system, can steer our course in the right direction and help us evaluate our personal progress along that way. But wait. There's a catch. The act of comparison isn't without its inaccuracies. Blind acceptance of its advice can lead you down wrong turns and dead ends and, in some cases, cause you to totally miss what's right in front of your eyes. All it takes is a temporary signal loss to detour into someone else's lane. And we all know how that ends.

Upgrading your GPS with a more intuitive signal reading can make reception clearer and speedier, helping you to keep on track without having to second-guess where you are headed or panicking when the annoying voice gives you last-minute notice of an upcoming turn. This allows you to reconnect with your more mindful self – the intuitive driver with the 360-degree vision that knows exactly where she's going.

According to many of our early philosopher friends (both West and East), intuition is the most immediate way of knowing – a reliable shortcut to your fuel tank of self-knowledge. Take that, Google! What's more, intuition usually travels with its trusty navigator, instinct, and has a canny knack of interpreting this sense of knowing in the body. You know the feeling: a knot in the stomach, a tingle of inspiration, a heavy heart. That's instinct's handiwork. The best part? The knowing one gets from intuition – that instant feeling that tells you if you are on the right path. To receive the signal, however, you need to be tuned in.

More often than not, we allow our maximising backseat driver to lead the way, overruling intuition's roadmap. This fella doesn't do feelings and can be quite an avoidant character (hence why he never asks for directions). As a result, we go round in circles, not really making any progress. Your task is to quieten the voice of maximising anxiety with the calming tones of intuition and to arrive at a middle path, rather than getting stuck on the 'shoulda, woulda, coulda' of your journey.

Note: the first answer that comes to mind usually arrives compliments of your internal guidance system, intuition. Allowing your inner maximiser's logic to take the wheel usually results in looking through the rear-view mirror and a long-winded explanation as to where you went wrong, what turn you should have taken and why you should've listened to him in the first place. The choice is yours: short and sweet or rambling explanation? Thought so.

Consider the exercise that follows a toolbox tip that can be used anywhere, any time – useful when pressed for time or resetting our emotional co-ordinates. Try it before any potentially incendiary social situations (meeting the in-laws, blind dates, flying it solo to a wedding) or every once in a while to keep you aligned with the bigger picture and what brings you satisfaction. Wheel Spinner, take notes. This next section is for you!

Feeling the Signal

Intuition may be a solid GPS but all it takes is the odd mind-flap to interfere with the signal. You can blame it on the amygdala

– the brain's own Chicken Little. Housed in the limbic brain, where feelings of environmental danger and safety reside, the amygdala is a sensitive soul and, given the right conditions, can generate next-level dread about things that haven't even happened yet. Panic merchant? Perhaps, but she's just doing her job. Her fear-based belief that the sky will fall sets off the limbic alarm bells if there's a mere whiff of danger in the offing. This, in turn, releases the fight-or-flight hormone cortisol to help us cope with an imminent (or non-existent) threat. Over time, the repeated release of cortisol (and this bird's apocalyptic talk) exhausts the nervous system, leading to indelible changes in the grey matter. In other words, what you focus on grows. So unless living in the horrors excites you, it might be time to swap that wing-flapping for an exercise in calm.

Let's start with a visualisation exercise to identify and clear up any underlying feelings that can scramble our navigation signal.

For this exercise, you'll need a notebook, a pen and a quiet space where you can spend 10 minutes alone without being interrupted – a park bench, the attic, the cleaning cupboard (let's face it – no one goes in there!).

• Close your eyes, take a deep breath and say the words 'my life'. Allow your conscious mind to build a picture of where you are at present. Hold the image in your head and see what feelings come up.

71

- Write down any fear-based emotions that come to mind. Don't allow your inner editor to tweak and spell-check this technique – uncensored is best.
- Check in with your body. How do these emotions feel? Where do they sit – in your neck, chest, gut? Stay with the discomfort. Be curious about why and when it happens. Maybe your tummy does a backflip when you compare your salary to that of your peers, or maybe your throat tightens when asked about your future plans.
- Next to each emotion, write a small explanation (one sentence) as to why it has come up. Studies have shown that the simple act of labelling a feeling lowers its activation in the amygdala. Consider it lexical Rescue Remedy: by indexing and filing each emotion, you're clearing the mental clutter and creating cognitive calm. Ahhhhh ...

Next, review your statements:

- Ask yourself what word or words sum up these statements.
- Check in with those words. How does they sound? Are they liberating or do they feel like a stretch? If your fear-based feelings are still doing the Funky Chicken dance and singing 'The Sky Is Falling', then ease off and find a reframe word that feels more appropriate.
- Now, rewrite your story with a happy medium statement starting with the word 'I'. Make sure to use emotive language (for example: love, enjoy, desire), which is known to have an effect on the subconscious mind. As mentioned in

Chapter 2, the subconscious is crazy gullible, so this is your chance to tell it what you want it to hear, not what others have been telling you.

- Finally, read your happy medium statements aloud. Tune into how they feel. Nice, right? Repeat, repeat, repeat until they form little grooves of goodness in your head.

Feeling out of GPS range? I'll start us off. It's always me, isn't it?

The examples below represent the areas in my life that tend to ignite when I get too close to the naked flame of comparison. Hey, even so-called expert inexperts have their weaknesses. With a wee bit of subliminal subterfuge, I can easily get back to the present without presenting for third-degree self-esteem burns at A&E. This keeps me from endlessly ruminating or indulging in negative self-talk, which only serves to block the present tense and put the future on hold.

FEELING	REASON	REFRAME
Embarrassed	I still only have my learner's permit and don't have a car.	I am lucky that I don't need a car living in the city. Everything I need is on my doorstep. I can take my test when I'm ready.
Anxious	I make less money than my peers.	I am fortunate to do something I adore for a living. Job satisfaction is very important to me.

FEELING	REASON	REFRAME
Worried	I still rent and haven't got on the property ladder yet.	I love where I live. Not being tied to a mortgage means less worry and stress, especially given my work is freelance.
Insecure	I am single and haven't settled down yet.	I enjoy my own company and I'm not in a relationship for the sake of it.
Reframe word: Freedom		
Happy medium statement: I love my life because of the freedom it gives me.		

The next time someone moves the goal posts or drops a humble-brag bomb, tune into your GPS signal and remind yourself of why you are satisfied with where you are. The beauty of intuition? It strengthens with practice. The more you engage it, the easier you'll find that feel-good frequency. Before long, it'll become second nature and your subconscious will assign a preset button to this sense of satisfaction. Handy little hack, no? Why not take it for a test drive? See how it feels. The closer you get acquainted with your happy medium, the easier it'll be to tell the story of who you are, as opposed to who you think you should be. And that's got to feel good. So start stocking up on all the feels, kiddos, because the next chapter takes this dual-lens approach to self-reflection that bit deeper. Are you ready? Now, say 'cheese'!

Happiness Hacks

THE HALO EFFECT

Excuse me, Mr Clooney. Is that a steaming cup of Nespresso in your hand or are you just happy to see me? All kidding aside, it's no coincidence that our morning coffee tastes infinitely superior when we believe we're sampling the same beans as Hollywood royalty. Psychologist Edward Lee Thorndike dubbed this phenomenon 'the halo effect' – where a single element can (positively or negatively) subconsciously skew our perception of the big picture, something which advertising boffins know oh-so-well. Remember: a halo doesn't have too far to fall to become a noose. So don't choke under the pressure of buying into a lifestyle by association, be it a celebrity endorsement or an influencer's fine-tuned Instagram feed. Happiness, after all, is an inside job.

Good for: Eternal Bachelor, Something Better, Neighbourhood Watch

THE CONNECTION CONUNDRUM

Here's a challenge for all Facebook fans. The next time you log on to your account, make a note as to the reason why. Next to each reason, clarify whether the action taken was passive or active. In other words, did you actively message a friend, leave a comment or engage in a conversation? Or

75

did you only scan walls, snoop on photographs and stalk newsfeeds? According to a 2010 study carried out at the Human-Computer Institute at Carnegie Mellon, passive consumption of Facebook correlates with feelings of disconnectedness and a marginal increase in depression, with more satisfaction reported from making that extra dollop of effort. The takeaway? Instead of using Facebook as a distraction or for watching your 'like' counts rise, why not engage directly with those you have accepted as 'friends'? Ya know, like in real life.

Good for: Eternal Bachelor, Something Better, Neighbourhood Watch

ALLABOUTME.COM

What do the internet and the phrase 'too much information' have in common?

Everything.

The biggest cause of anti-social behaviour online? A lack of boundaries. According to a peer-reviewed study carried out by Princeton and Freie Universität researchers, we spend approximately 30% of face-to-face conversations talking about ourselves, whereas this number jumps to 80% online. The lack of social cues like apoplectic faces, lobotomised stares and raised eyebrows makes it easier for us to go rogue with a narcissistic monologue or way-too-personal information. If in doubt, remember: behave the same online as you would offline. In other words, don't dominate the virtual airspace with a one-sided conversation. And put the skids on self-disclosure while you're at it. Ask yourself 'why' before you go TMI.

Good for: All types

MAKE TIME FOR IRL

Social networks are best used as a supplement to rather than a substitute for real-life interactions. Use to facilitate more face-time and you're onto a winner; use in lieu of face-time and you've lost the opportunity to strengthen existing or new connections and create stronger offline bonds. This particularly applies to online dating. As my wise friend Andy maintains, 'It's all about traffic. You've got to encourage footfall by making the effort and taking it offline.' Before you swipe right, ask yourself, 'Am I doing this for an ego boost or am I looking for an actual date?'

Good for: All types

CHAPTER 4

Selfies and the Authentic Self

Selfie-Documentation

I find that kind of 'look at me' narcissism terribly inconsiderate. If you need attention that badly, set yourself on fire.

JOAN RIVERS, *I HATE EVERYONE ... STARTING WITH ME*

Selfies. We don't give them enough credit. Back when the one-hour photo was the height of sophistication, getting a decent likeness involved a third party with a steady hand, a prayer to St Anthony and one shot to get it right. Self-documentation was raw at best. Mouths gaped, eyes squinted and limbs disappeared behind ill-timed shadows. All it took was one overblown flash to make it look like you'd stuck your head out the window of a moving car. A life futureproofed from comments such as 'I don't know which side of the family she gets that double chin from' meant taking control of the situation.

No one was safe. Reputation management entailed tactics such as intercepting prints at the local chemist and reefing out any offending anomalies. Adopting a wait-and-see policy was unconscionable. Not unless you fancied being framed, hung up and used as an ice-breaker at family gatherings. And to think, we've suffered years of such humiliation – until now.

The double-helix rise of front-facing camera phones and selfie culture since the early noughties has put the control squarely back in our hands. No more relying on Aunt Gertrude to capture your knowing Mona Lisa-esque expression from the right angle and with decent low lighting. Individual agency aided by technical wizardry means that now *we* craft the image – the mask we want others to see. The playing field has officially been levelled. Or has it?

The modern-day selfie has become more than its (duck) face value would suggest. Its prolific appeal across nations and generations has spawned both a growth industry (flying-drone selfie-sticks, anyone?) and a de facto cultural movement. Even the Dalai Lama and His Holiness have got in on the act. Most of all, the selfie has become a major production – one where the goal is capturing attention rather than capturing a moment. The fact that we're both the star of the show *and* its director, producer, lighting crew, glam squad, editing and post-production teams, set designer, props manager, runner, best boy and tea lady means contending with more options, more decisions and, ultimately, less satisfaction when our expectations (sunkissed skin and bedroom eyes) don't match the reality (sunburned skin and bloodshot eyes).

Choice, as we've come to know her, can be quite the demanding diva. No cut-rate champagne in her dressing room. No, ma'am. Only chilled Cristal served with titanium bendy straws. Wherever there's a whiff of 'could do better', there's an extreme makeover app offering a two-finger drag to smooth out wrinkles and facial features, and fancy doodads that make eyes rounder, chins shorter and smiles wider – all in the click of a 16-megapixel selfie flash. Why look like the best version of yourself when you can look like someone else? Gisele's legs? Don't mind if I do. The waist of Dita von Teese? Lay it on me, sister! The age of bricolage has officially dawned. Could this *get* any better?

Apparently so. No one bothers to read the fine print, do they? We may *think* we control our public personas but the selfie is essentially a co-production. It's no accident, in fact, that the word *persona* (what we know as our perceived image) is defined as 'a character adopted by an author or actor'. And like any performer, the public personas we create with our selfies need an audience to create an impression, to engage with and to compel others to like and to share. Feedback, after all, is the selfie's raison d'être. Without it, could the selfie even be said to exist? Cue: existentialist dilemma.

Think about it:

- Have you ever felt like shouting 'Well, dip me in chocolate and call me delicious!' because your selfie received a stellar number of likes or comments?
- Have you ever deleted your selfie in a fit of Linda Blair-style pique because it didn't elicit enough likes or comments?
- Have you ever found yourself humming 'The Sound of Silence' while waiting for your selfie to ping with its first like or comment?
- Have you ever had a full-scale diva head-spin and insisted on approving your precious mug in a group selfie?
- Have you ever asked that the offending shot is taken again … and again … and again?
- Have you ever left skid marks on your laptop in a bid to untag yourself from the offending shot before it's made its way onto friends' Facebook feeds?

Fear not. We all have, give or take a few dramatic gestures. As humans, our innate drive to bond and form communities means the brain is hardwired to respond more actively to faces than things; and our latent disposition to be noticed plays an equally important role, both of which explain the selfie's unerring appeal. In case you've forgotten about our friend dopamine, he's in on the act too. In fact, he's goading us on as we preen, pose and post, rewarding us with spikes of pleasure each time we take the mic and entertain the masses. And here's the sucker-punch. A recent study carried out by Harvard researchers has demonstrated that this activation in the brain peaks further still when people are aware of an audience. In other words, we play to the crowd. Ouch!

That might go a long way to explaining why since 2012, selfies have increased by an estimated 17,000%; and why in 2014, Android users alone posted 93 million selfies *per day*. Such is our craving for attention (and attendant distraction levels) that since 2015 alone, more people have died in pursuit of the perfect selfie than have been killed by shark attacks. Would you risk falling off a cliff or a bridge, touching live wires or being gored by a wild animal to get that perfect shot? Admit it. You hesitated for a second there. So what gives?

We're keen as mustard to make a ~~good~~ great impression, that's what. It was Canadian-American sociologist and writer Erving Goffman who first explored the concept of impression management in his 1959 bestseller *The Presentation of Self in Everyday Life*. According to Goffman, we are all 'performing' on the social stage, whether consciously or unconsciously. In other words, what we present to others (our audience) is designed to form an 'impression' or a desirable image. How we manage these impressions is carried out in three ways:

- Authentically: how we see ourselves
- Ideally: the way we wish we were
- Tactically: how others want or expect us to be.

Human nature being what it is, we're likely to tick all three boxes in how we present ourselves in our daily lives (List Maker, this should please you). Too much of any one impression, though, can get tangled in our maximising potential, ignite our capacity for compulsive comparison and, ultimately, affect our baseline satisfaction.

Compound this with an itchy trigger finger and, what do you know, suddenly we've become CEO of our own PR firm, managing the way people see us, when they see us (peak online traffic times, obviously) and how often. When it comes to creating an image, it's always the audience who gets the front row, leaving authenticity to crane its head from the cheap seats. Our goal? To discover just what type of impression we're making in the name of selfie expression. Let's find out, shall we?

Selfie Expression

The Situational Selfie relies on the context of place to tell its story. Often used to document an event or capture a moment that resonates with both subject and audience. Frequently taken at birthdays, weddings, gigs, sightseeing and while bucket-listing in remote parts of the world. Cleverly co-opted by Blatant Boasters looking to show off rather than share.

The Relational Selfie relies on the context of people to tell its story. Often used to share a connection or rapport with both subject and audience. Frequently taken in pairs (ussie), groups of friends and family (groufie) or with romantic partners (relfie). The preferred approach of Name Droppers looking to gain social capital with someone of a perceived higher status.

The Transformational Selfie relies on the context of inspiration to tell its story. Often used to showcase positive lifestyle changes and/or their physical effects. Frequently taken with a salad, green juice (btw, seaweed is the new kale), random health supplement (100% organic baobab fruit powder, any takers?) or in the presence of intimidating gym equipment. Adopted customarily by Image Crafters to put some 'grand' in their standing.

The Promotional Selfie relies on the context of an event to tell its story. Often used to raise awareness of a charity, cause, new business venture, product launch or personal achievement. Frequently taken with transparency but prone to misappropriation by Humble Braggers orchestrating impression-management campaigns.

The Mirror Image Selfie relies on the context of the self to tell its story. Often used as a means of self-evaluation, indexing a moment for future reference or demonstrating different sides to one's personality. Frequently taken in the bathroom, gym, bedroom, department-store changing-room or any place bearing a reflective surface. Can sometimes be mistaken for the Daddy Issues Selfie if in the absence of clothing.

The Best Self Selfie relies on the context of idealism to tell its story. Often used as a means of self-benchmarking, for use on dating sites and/or maintaining one's public appearance. Frequently taken on good hair days, good outfit days and/or good make-up days. Indirectly appropriated by Image Crafters with a well-placed hashtag such as #wokeuplikethis, #bedhead or #realme.

The Danger: High Voltage Selfie relies on gross acts of extremism to tell its story. Often used as a means of showcasing one's fearlessness and impunity in the face of danger. Frequently taken in compromising situations, including but not limited to: at the mouth of a volcano, on top of a crane, on the edge of a cliff, in proximity to a wild animal. Extolled by Blatant Boasters as evidence of self-styled prowess.

The 'Oh No, They Didn't!' Selfie relies on gross acts of stupidity to tell its story. With zero purpose other than to showcase an egregious lack of self-awareness, such selfies are frequently taken at funerals, accidents, crime scenes, hijacking scenarios (not making this up), with weapons, in front of oncoming vehicles or – wait for it – after sex. Oh no, they didn't! Oh yes, they did.

The Daddy Issues Selfie relies on flagrant acts of attention-seeking to tell its story. Often used as a means of sexual validation and to put a plaster on the burst pipe of self-esteem. Frequently taken in scanty underwear, butt-naked or by showcasing a body part such as the cleavage (boobie), chest (chestie), bicep (flexie) or gluteus maximus (belfie). Its scion? None other than Mrs Kim Kardashian-West, purveyor of the existential quip, 'Nude selfies until I die.'

Did you catch that glare? Might it be coming from your selfie-reflection? Sadly, the mirror of truth isn't equipped with a dimmer switch or #lo-fi filter when we face up to our foibles. That's the thing about self-expression: with little provocation, it can easily parlay self-promotion. Not that there's anything wrong with shining a light on your latest Prada shoes every once in a while – we all love a bit of a nose into the lives of others (just ask Neighbourhood Watch). That said, enough 'oohs' and 'aahs' from your audience can make casually indulgent posts a well-shod habit. Before you know it, you're doped up on dopamine, looking for your next virtual validation. A bit of selfie-awareness goes a long way.

If creating a happy medium involves balance, then establishing a reciprocal value between the self(ie) and its audience should be top of our agenda. Knowing your angles and finding the light is all well and good but so is being real and relatable. People want to see themselves in you, not just you in you. Masks may add drama but they also hide the real person beneath, flaws and all. On the other hand, extreme self-disclosure can be equally off-putting – like your boss telling you about his messy divorce at the Christmas party. Too much information leads to overexposure, leaving you to look totally washed out. We'll get to this in just a few.

First, let's figure out what your selfie is telling the world. Is it a well-rehearsed, spin-tastic Best Self answer or is it more of a verbal vomit, 'Oh No, They Didn't!' spew-fest? Either way, you've got the power to rewrite your story and make it more character-driven, rather than an 'all about me' monologue. As discovered in Chapter 3, the luxury of social media is in making a first impression twice. You want in? Then it's time to give your selfies a fresh point of view.

The Point-of-View Finder

Right then. Let's put this into focus. The point-of-view finder, much like the previous exercises, uses the past to gain clarity on our present direction. In observing your selfie history, the aim of this process is:

- To highlight patterns of behaviours that could be at odds with your personal satisfaction
- To get clarity on your selfie motivation by accessing autobiographical memories.

Quick neuroscience 101: autobiographical memories tell the who, what, where and when of our personal experiences and are housed in a part of the brain called the hippocampus, which functions to create the story of the self. When we look back on photos, we are in effect recalling a life event and the emotions that came with it. In channelling the past, we're better able to understand what motivates us to behave in certain ways and, if necessary, how to change this orientation for a happier present.

Remember: be easy on your selfie. So you've got over three hundred Mirror Images that could rival Narcissus on a good day. Maybe your decision-making skills weren't exactly on point the day you posed with the corpse at your great-uncle

Ralph's wake. No one's judging here (eh, well, maybe just a bit). The objective with the point-of-view finder is to become an impartial observer of your actions and thus more selfie-aware. Are we good? Good. Now, get ready for your close-up!

First, take a sample (say, four) of the most recent selfies on your phone, laptop or tablet. Grab your notebook and pen and map out the following:

- **Selfie:** A bit about the image in question
- **Selfie expression:** For example, Mirror Image, 'Oh No, They Didn't!'
- **Impression type:** Authentic, ideal or tactical
- **Motivation:** The reason for taking it – be honest!
- **Feeling:** The emotional driver behind taking it

Use this format for each of your four selfies, filling in the details that best describe each one. Now look for the patterns across impression types and motivation. What do you notice? Is it all 'me me me' or is there a shared connection with your audience?

For example, when *The Happy Closet* was published, I admittedly took many a tactical selfie of my hardback baby and me: at home, in bookstores, in restaurants, at the pub. In fact, I asked all of my readers to do the same and with that, created a wall of 'book shelfies' on the blog section of my website, www.thehappycloset.me. Strategic, sure; but the reward was reciprocal for both my audience and me as we shared the experience together. Plus, it was great to connect and thank those who had contributed to the book's success. In short, my motivation was transparent (promote the book), involved my audience (let's do this together) and it encoded a memory I'll always cherish. Ahhh ...

That's not to say I haven't been party to my fair share of selfie-destructive habits – just take a look at this chapter's Confession Corner. Nonetheless, the selfie cross-section below builds a visual of what *could* happen when the point-of-view finder gets a bit blurry and/or when Pinot Grigio is involved. Before casting any aspersions, please note that I take no responsibility for this clanger. I do strongly recommend a bowl of popcorn and a comfy seat, however; it's a good 'un!

Disclaimer: The following scene contains sexual references and some scenes that have been made for entertainment purposes only. Any resemblance to those living (or dead) is purely coincidental.

SELFIE	SELFIE EXPRESSION	IMPRESSION	MOTIVATION	FEELING
Bridesmaid at best friend's wedding	Mirror Image	Ideal	To solicit feedback. Was feeling attractive and needed a boost after recent break-up with boyfriend.	Confident
Photo with (hot) best man at best friend's wedding	Situational	Ideal	'You look so cute together!' everyone said. Feels nice to be back in a couple.	Secure

89

SELFIE	SELFIE EXPRESSION	IMPRESSION	MOTIVATION	FEELING
Kissing (hot) best man at best friend's wedding	Relational	Tactical	OK, so things progressed pretty fast here (I blame the free bar). I won't lie: my ex still follows me on Facebook so I left it up to make him jealous.	Insecure
After-sex selfie with (hot) best man in the hotel at best friend's wedding	'Oh No, They Didn't'	Tactical	What's the old saying – 'You get over one guy by getting under another'? Just in case my ex didn't see the first 50 selfies of me looking amazing with another man, this one ought to do it. Too far? Maybe?	Desperate

Wowsers! That didn't end well. Albeit extreme, this cautionary tale illustrates how things can quickly go awry in the name of selfie expression. Let's look at the playback.

Ranging from ideal to tactical impressions, our selfie taker is focused on the way she wants to be perceived by a certain someone. It's not that she's looking to share her rom-com character arc and post-coital cuddles with the internet. Her interest is in the potential reward (the remote chance of her ex seeing them and/or being overcome with jealousy) that exposing them to the worldwide web will elicit – even if that does involve maximum self-disclosure. Risky business, no? Let's dig a bit deeper and discover why.

Psychologists refer to this phenomenon as the 'cognitive disconnect' – a condition whereby the brain disassociates from a particular action. In behavioural economics, the term is applied to the sense of non-spending we feel when we use a credit card. In social media, the term can be applied to the disconnect we experience when posting personal information on the net. Put simply, we're quick to post a bikini shot for potentially thousands of people online but we wouldn't dream of walking to the shops for the Sunday paper in our bikini. You see?

This would have been a good time for our errant bridesmaid to use the feeling the signal exercise from Chapter 3. By tuning into her intuition, she could have saved herself a full-body dive from confidence to desperation. Why? Because she wouldn't have allowed her self-esteem to be tied up in the image. Ergo, she wouldn't have lost sight of her point of view. Deepak, move over, my friend – there's room on this sofa for two!

Although we do sometimes consciously make choices that don't serve our best interests, more often than not our habitual behaviour happens by default and without our permission. Remember the basal ganglia, our productive PA from Chapter 1? In a bid to save cognitive juice, she's automated all non-essential tasks, which includes your daily selfie habit. That might explain why you've never realised how many Relational Selfies you post of you and your better half – it's become an unconscious automatic behaviour. It's all well and good to be proud of your gorgeous arm candy but if the reward is linked to feedback on the image rather than the relationship itself, it might be worth adjusting your depth of field. A shallow focus only serves the person in the foreground. Go deeper if you want a more inclusive shot.

See what I'm getting at? If most of your selfies are Mirror Image, why not add a few Situational ones to create context on your visual journey? Already pretty balanced? Good for you. Go forth and self-document – mindfully, of course. For those of you with a penchant for Photoshop and other WiFi-enabled wizardry, stay put. I've got a bone to pick with you. But before I do ...

Confession Corner

'Ohhhhh, that's good. Really good. A little to the left. Just there. Yep, a bit more. That's it. Keep going. Don't be gentle now. Try just inside the thigh. And along my knees. Don't forget my bottom. That needs serious work. Make sure you go at it good and proper now.'

The above is an extract from my first up-close-and-personal encounter with retouching. To preface, I had just started working in fashion as a stylist and was asked to be on the other side of the camera for a modelling cameo. Although relatively happy in my own skin, I felt as if I had been slapped with the wet fish of insecurity. A photoshoot with me in it? The pressure was suddenly on. I didn't feel ready, much less camera-ready. So I spent two weeks preparing for my close-up by binging on fruit and cardio (loose translation: drinking wine and watching *EastEnders* while attached to a SlenderTone slimming belt) in a last-ditch effort to evict the spare tyre that had claimed squatter's rights along my midsection.

Post-photoshoot, I'm sitting with the photographer reviewing the shots when he mentions something about smoothing out a few things. Smooth? Or did he say 'remove'? This, of course, I interpreted as a tummy tuck, liposuction, a set of sculpted abs, a thigh gap, a butt you could rest a drink on and a side of fries. Like any good doctor dealing with a deluded patient, he didn't carry out my demands. A bit of brightening and lightening, perhaps, but not the full-scale archaeological dig I had in mind. Just as well there was a responsible adult in charge. Had it been me, I would have been bandying that 3D magic wand like the evil genius in a Marvel comic. Caption: 'When great power falls into the wrong hands.' *Mwahahahahhhh!*

Fast-forward about 10 years to our digitally-enhanced culture. What used to be the sole remit of art directors and advertisers has now become part and parcel of our democratic selfie society. Downloadable social media apps that promise retouching and airbrushing have fogged up the lens through which our personal story is communicated. Unlike the glossy magazine spreads that, we are suspiciously aware, utilise the fantasy of Photoshop, there's a scarier subterfuge at play in the constructed reality of social media. Suddenly, we've all got the tools and, importantly, the reward to become the Best Self version of ourselves – even if it isn't in our own best interests.

Such is the paradox of personal power: when the weight of having it all includes having the perfect body, the temptation to cast ourselves in a flattering photographic light can turn us into digital Dr Frankensteins. We've all seen the horror stories: thigh gaps that have taken a bite out of someone's vulva; boob jobs that resemble inflated car airbags; and the heavy-handed airbrushing that makes its victims look like wax dummies. I should know. My inner feminist whacks me repeatedly with a copy of *The Beauty Myth* every time I think of how willing I was to go rogue and replace my entire body in that very instance. Oh, and my happy medium with it.

That's the thing about peer pressure: you wind up ditching your authentic self on the off-chance the cool kids will let you sit with them at lunch. Technology has only served to magnify this impulse, which, in a weird way, might well be a good thing – it might help us recognise the latent insecurities that play havoc with our happy medium. The gap we need to address isn't between our legs; it's the one between who we are and who we think we should be. That's where expectation lives and disappointment thrives.

Instead of playing the evil genius, how about donning a bad-ass cape and being your own superhero? Apart from the mad craic you'd have wearing a telepathic tiara and wielding a lasso of truth, you could be a not-so-secret agent of social media change. The decision is in your hands. Go on, look at it. That 5.5-inch diagonal device to which you are permanently attached? Its potential is at once transformative and talismanic, acting as both a weapon and a shield. With it, you are bulletproof, provided you are prepared to make like Wonder Woman and choose not to be a victim of unattainable beauty standards. A superhero doesn't point the finger unless, of course, it emits some sort of rad laser beam of justice. Then that's totally allowed.

The upshot of playing the superhero? You've got the power to bestow your selfies with a new meaning: one that will encourage others to create their own happy medium. Tapping into this wellspring of meaning isn't impossible but it does require a healthy disregard for the status quo – a new aesthetic normal. Put it this way: you're not doing your sisters (or brothers) any favours by pinching and stretching that retina screen to make your waist look like it can fit behind an A4 sheet of paper. Do the decent thing and lay off the sleight of hand. Instead, use the arsenal of happiness hacks on the following pages to deactivate the expectations that play mind games with personal satisfaction – not just for your selfie but for everyone else's too. Make your goal to be happy with what you've got. You'll see why in the next chapter.

Selfie-Reflection

When Naomi Woolf published *The Beauty Myth* in 1991, she exposed the not-so-lovely effects of beauty advertising on women's self-esteem. Most of all, she called bullsh*t on the 'have it all' attitude perpetuated in glossy magazines, the crazy aspirational tone that grew in tandem with increasingly unattainable images of the ideal woman. Food and weight preoccupations became the kryptonite that stripped women of our control and, to a great degree, still are. No one would have predicted the social media revolution that would unfold in the next decade but Woolf did foreshadow an inconvenient truth: although we may be more upwardly mobile than our mothers and grandmothers, we're not doing ourselves any favours in caving to a currency that trades solely on physical worth. At the time Wolf was writing *The Beauty Myth*, women did not have the power to directly affect the images that were being presented to them. That, thankfully, has changed. We are in a position now to create a new reality – one that will bring us closer to a happy medium; we just need to lay off the retouching sauce a bit. In the words of comedian, writer, actress, producer and all-round Renaissance woman Tina Fey, 'Photoshop itself is not evil. Just like Italian salad dressing is not inherently evil, until you rub it all over a desperate young actress and stick her on the cover of *Maxim*, pretending to pull her panties down.' Mic drop.

Happiness Hacks

KEEP IT TO YOUR-SELFIE

Nothing warrants an 'unfollow' more than conspicuous oversharing. In the interests of proper selfie etiquette, it's therefore advisable to find your filter – not those on your social media apps but rather the one on your pesky trigger finger. Give yourself a privacy calorie count – a daily posting cap to keep you from overindulging. Make like porridge and operate a slow-release policy. A selfie fest only puts others in a carb coma. Don't be that person. The middle ground – that's what we're aiming for.

Good for: Neighbourhood Watch, Mystic Meg

REWRITE THE SCRIPT

Take a revisionist approach to your selfie history. Look through your visual archives and examine if the images collectively tell a story. It's a great way of remembering and recontextualising events. Ask yourself: what is the story arc? Who are the characters? If you are the only character and there is absolutely no plot, you may want to reconsider your point of view. Better still, go one step further and retag each selfie with an authentic caption. Looking so good you could eat yourself? Great. Now let everyone know it took two hours, three pairs of false eyelashes, four silent prayers and 35 frames to get that shot. Truth, as they say, is sometimes stranger (and more interesting) than fiction.

Good for: All types

MAKE NORMAL THE NEW NORMAL

Looking camera-ready may make us feel good, but taking candid shots can make *others* feel good and create a curious immediacy in terms of bonding. The growing trend for debunking the myth of the 'perfect' female form has bred more authenticity on the net. Postpartum stretch-marks, real thigh selfies and body-positive messages have created new tribes of realness in which multiple definitions of body norms are, well, normal. While you're at it, create a new set of trending hashtags and lead your own feel-good movement #everybodyisbeautiful #lovemylovehandles #allbodiesaregoodbodies #thisisnotasparetyreitisafueltank foralovemachine

Good for: Eternal Bachelor, Something Better, Neighbourhood Watch

SMILE, DAMMIT!

We love to pout. Fact. That said, the internet is fast beginning to resemble a zoo with fish gape, sparrow face and duck lips standard selfie fare. Animal-inspired poses are a mug's game and could be swapped for a much more effective expression. A smile, as scientific evidence supports, is contagious and helps instil feelings of happiness, so why not spread the love? In the words of Dolly Parton in *Steel Magnolias*, 'Smile. It increases your face value.' While you're at it, stand up straight and leave the pigeon toes to the pigeons.

Good for: All types

FIND FAULT IN THE DEFAULT

Partial to a peace sign? Love a good bikini shot, even if it is pelting horizontal rain? If you've got a selfie habit, chances are you've got a default too. Often this is linked to a compliment or a feeling (sexy, strong) that makes us fall for its sweet talk over and over again. The trick? Ask yourself how you'd feel without it. Exposed? Incomplete? Sit with that ambiguity; allow yourself to feel uncomfortable. Then make like Buddha and practice some healthy non-attachment. In other words, don't be so fixated with the end result. Selfies can distract us by pulling us out of the present moment. Adopt some perspective. Allow for life's perfect imperfections; accept them and move on to more important things.

Good for: Frequent Trader, Eternal Bachelor, Something Better

BE INSPIRED

Media psychologist Pamela Rutledge suggests taking a selfie with something that inspires gratitude or accesses your sweet spot. As your memories of experiences are stored in multiple neural networks, revisiting an image can access that moment in time, not to mention the feelings that accompany it. Tip? Close your eyes and sit with the feelings these special selfies evoke. Let that butterscotch bliss bubble over until you can practically taste it. By capturing a moment instead of seeking attention, the feeling will stay with you longer. Feel and repeat each time life decides to banjax your happy medium.

Good for: All types

QUESTION FACE VALUE

In the land of social media, perception is nine-tenths of the law. In other words, face value rules supreme. In the interests of storytelling, the narrator will embellish, polish and edit that face where necessary. Your job? To question the reliability of the first-person point of view. Blind acceptance means we often don't see the 'wonderful' Oz pulling the levers. Make like Toto and pull back the curtains.

Always ask: is this totally objective or have some scenarios been constructed for our viewing pleasure? There's nothing wrong with a bit of hocus pocus, provided you're not hypnotised by the act.

Good for: Neighbourhood Watch, Something Better, Eternal Bachelor

LIMIT YOUR MIRRORS

Sociologist Charles Horton Cooley, who coined the Looking Glass theory, maintains that our identities develop through the perception of others – namely, the circles of friends and acquaintances with whom we surround ourselves. Although it's understandable that reflected appraisals account for much of how we view ourselves, the sphere of those who influence our sense of identity shouldn't extend to thousands of folk you wouldn't know from a bar of soap. Rarely does approval by committee ever serve the individual, even if the consensus is a thumbs-up. External validation may feel good in the moment, but too much of a good thing can lead to trading off on your self-esteem for the sake of a quick ego boost.

Good for: All types

CHAPTER 5

Living the Good Life

The Easy Life: The Story of More

Life is simple. It's just not easy.

STEVE MARABOLI, *UNAPOLOGETICALLY YOU: REFLECTIONS ON LIFE AND THE HUMAN EXPERIENCE*

E xcuse me. Hi there. I know you're busy pretending not to watch YouTube videos during work time but this will only take a few minutes. I want to share some information with you that literally has the power to change your life.

First, let me ask you a simple question. How would you feel about a lifestyle of flexibility and freedom – personally and financially? Think about it. No 9–5 job, no commute, no boss, no trading hours for money – no trade-offs at all, just a limitless passive income and tonnes of free time. In fact, I'm chatting to you now from a pedalo cocktail bar in the middle of the Arabian

Sea! Cool, right? This isn't just a dream; it's the life you bloody well deserve. Why not grab it with both hands and change your remarkably unfulfilled reality? There's no experience necessary and the pay-off is mind-blowing. In fact, I'm *so* committed to helping you harness your untapped potential that I've developed a free, yes, FREE audio course to guide you in living a life of totally unattainable indulgence (well, the first 30 seconds are free. You'll need to pony up €199.99 to access the other 19 and a half minutes). Sounds like freedom, though, doesn't it? Of course it does. Great, let's get the ball rolling then, shall we? MasterCard, Visa or PayPal?

If only the path to happiness were as simple as an infomercial sales pitch. One click and we'd all be on the way to our bliss – the lives of instant harmony we were meant to lead. But life satisfaction demands a bit more from us than handing over our credit-card details in the vain hope of receiving an abundance cheque from the universe. Empty wins and overnight successes may be seductive but they're also way too easy. For lasting happiness, most of us need to feel the total absorption of a challenge, the experience of the journey en route to our desired destination. But what happens when we're pursuing the wrong thing or going in the wrong direction? What if the dream we're chasing is out of our reach – and with good reason? What then?

We've already seen how digital interruptions can scupper our decision-making prowess. Is it any wonder, then, that our penchant for distraction seeks refuge in the success stories of the insta-famous, the overnight entrepreneurs and 'the new rich'? We prefer not to entertain failures – their dinner conversation can be a bit of a drag. Instead, our focus squares on the faces of those who've made empires on a few euro and a big idea – the tastemakers, game-changers, trendsetters and market leaders who dared to win. We are captivated by the sheer potential of a limitless lifestyle, the ability to make an impression that says 'I made it and I made it big'.

Here's where our blue-sky mentality hits some cloudy patches. We don't always know what's best for us. In fact, we're undeniably rubbish at predicting our own happiness, as Harvard psychologist Daniel Gilbert explains in *Stumbling on Happiness*: 'Because most of us get so much more practice imagining good than bad events, we tend to overestimate the likelihood that good events will actually happen to us, which leads us to be unrealistically optimistic about our futures.' In short, we consistently mess up when making decisions that affect our future well-being. Remember the scratch-cards in Chapter 1? Stay tuned because there's another case of scratching coming right up. Getting back to business ...

How does this forecasting flub play out? For starters, we tend to focus on success stories while ignoring failures. Commonly referred to as 'survivorship bias', this cognitive error of fixating on life's visible winners and ignoring their less successful counterparts can make us prone to misplaced optimism about our own potential. Where this becomes an issue is when we interpret these stories to suit our personal narratives. The one-offs and one-shot deals become expectations for ourselves, our new gold standard, despite being unique examples. Consider it a bit like reading an array of horoscopes for your star sign but choosing only the good bits (love finds you in the supermarket, at the gym and in places where friends meet. How convenient!) and disregarding the rest. Not that I would do that, of course. Ahem.

Combine this inclination with a 'want it now' culture hooked on instant results and before long, we've set our personal goals on fast-forward too: the four-hour work week, the five-minute motivator, the 60-second life coach, 20 seconds to charisma, the osmosis method (absorb the life you want!). Our expectation of immediate gratification has generated a plethora of shortcuts to the so-called good life. 'Who wants to be a millionaire?' may well be the catchphrase of our generation. After all, 'Who wants to be a civil servant?' doesn't quite have the same ring. Poor Aristotle would be pitching a next-level hissy fit if he were here right now.

The real issue? We've all got a bang of notions about us. Yes, we do – myself included. Before you roll your eyes and mentally discount yourself from that description, it would help to understand that all of us are prone to what psychologists call the 'better than average' effect. This effect causes us to consistently overestimate our abilities, positive qualities and future potential. In other words, we rate ourselves highly. Our expectations are way off the charts (CEO of a multi-national and still in national school – why not?). Although there is scientific evidence to support the link between happiness and healthy self-esteem, too much of it is a recipe for dashed hopes and insidious entitlement. Being better than others is how we've come to define happiness – a semantic snafu that not only encourages excessive self-esteem (what we've come to know as narcissism) but that can also magnify the gap between our actual and ideal selves. The result? Disappointment when reality fails to deliver on the version of life we ordered.

You see, selecting poor role models, expecting instant results and overestimating our own abilities is just the kind of hokum that gets us all in a pickle. When it comes to making decisions that impact our happiness levels, it's very easy to fall prey to the fairy dust of potential when purpose requires a more considered cognitive load. Potential, after all, is a silky smooth operator, all white smiles and promises; while purpose prefers to read the fine print before signing over the keys to its happiness. You want to avoid being permanently disappointed? Setting satisfying (and achievable) goals – whether learning how to wakeboard or waking up next to Mr Right – is the cornerstone to kicking unrealistic expectations in the goolies and knocking notions on the head. If you'd like to craft a more rewarding storyline for yourself, then consider this cautionary tale before plotting your next move.

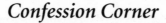

Confession Corner

When I was warned never to scratch someone else's patch (dubious recruitment double entendre for encroaching on someone else's territory), I knew it was time to leave. Bad timing, given I had just arrived. It was my second recruitment job (you heard about the first one in *The Happy Closet)* and was, most definitely, not in the plan. I came to London to find full-time work as a writer but due to a small issue with liquidity (loosely translated: arriving in the Big Smoke with a heavily pregnant credit card and the princely sum of €200), I was forced to park my pipe-dream until I started turning some coin.

Essentially, I lied to get basically the same job I left behind in Ireland. This entailed five interviews, five suits and a lot of talk about my 'scores on the doors'. I felt dirty – walk-of-shame dirty – each time I left my soon-to-be employer's West End offices, secretly hoping I wouldn't get hired; but I did. And so I found myself sequestered in a conference room on a three-day fast-track training course to get up to speed with how to overcome objections; how to seal a deal; how to wear a phone headset without looking like Britney Spears; how to be proactive and results-driven while staying on message; and how to keep my finger on the pulse in a company that expects its team to hit the ground running.

The only finger on the pulse was the one checking to see if I were still alive. The prospect of this being my future had me teetering on the edge of 'What have I done?' I had to keep reminding myself that it was only temporary (even though I just signed a full-time contract) and that my dream job at Vogue House was but a P60 away. I was, in industry-speak, a square peg in a round hole; the wrong person for the job; not on brand; the wearer of dead man's shoes. I knew I if I didn't get out of Dodge, I'd be dodging a fusillade of regrets on account of my poor choices.

I did get out of the human-chattel racket but never quite hit the editorial big time like I hoped, despite my bags of enthusiasm. It wasn't for lack of trying. I pushed for four and a half years and made myself miserable in the process. London didn't love me. She made it quite clear. So desperate was I to fill some foolish notion of bright lights and big city, I persisted and, well, she resisted. I survived (just about) but I sure as hell didn't thrive. My myopic view of the road ahead, inability to judge the terrain and blind insistence on staying the course taught me a lesson in humility and, by default, a masterclass in finding my flow.

Sometimes, the more satisfying route is the path of least resistance – not to be confused with taking the easy way out (unless you truly believe you can make €23,567.45 in one month by calling 1800-SUCKER). Creating life satisfaction isn't always about reaching for the stars, achieving peak performance or unleashing your inner cage fighter. More often than not, it's about doing what comes naturally, accessing that state of mind where time stands still and well-being takes you gently by the hand. Curious to know more? Let's find out, shall we?

Flow state

in the flow

in the groove

in the zone

feeling it

in your element

engrossed in something

inspired

clicking

engaged

holistic hustling

really into

digging it

going great guns

cruising

total immersion

complete absorption

singular focus

channelling

on the money

mushin no shin (無心の心)

zanshin (残心)

all about it

all over it

all over it like a fat kid on cake

locked and loaded

deep in thought

intent

mindful

rapt

connected

hyperfocused

on a roll

on your game

on point

on fire

on it like a car bonnet

cooking with gas

suckin' diesel

huzzah!

The Good Life: Going with the Flow

The point is, not to resist the flow.

HARUKI MURAKAMI, *THE WIND-UP BIRD CHRONICLE*

Going with the flow gets a bad rap. Often mistaken for herd mentality, complacency or the remit of Jimmy Buffet songs ('Wasted away again in Margaritaville!'), its meaning rarely holds company with that of productivity. But flow is more than a laidback epithet. It's the stealth samurai of satisfaction; the judo throw of good decisions; a secret attention weapon when distraction tries elbowing its way to the front of the queue.

Quick psychology 101: Hungarian psychologist and happiness pioneer Mihaly Csikszentmihalyi coined the term 'flow' to describe a state of total engagement and heightened awareness in the here and now, that moment of complete absorption in a challenging task that is well matched to your abilities. This can be anything from playing with your kid to playing the stock market, so long as your attention is present and accounted for. This is how flow's CV stacks up:

- Flow puts us in a good mood.
- Flow increases our psychological well-being.
- Flow adds meaning to our day-to-day existence.
- Flow is optimal experience (maximisers, rejoice!).
- Flow is the antidote to the easy life.

- Flow is reward in itself.
- Flow is satisfaction.
- Flow is presence – *with a cherry on top.*

Sweet, eh? What's even sweeter is how easily we can use flow to lay the groundwork for living the good life and finding our happy medium. The founder of the positive psychology movement, Martin Seligman, believes that achieving personal satisfaction boils down to a very simple principle: playing to your strengths. Not to be confused with talents (Mariah Carey's glass-shattering range, Usain Bolt's lightning speed), which you're born with, strengths are psychological characteristics that (like flow) must be acquired and cultivated. Whereas talents are automatic, strengths are voluntary and are therefore a by-product of our conscious choices.

We choose to tell a woman exiting a public bathroom that her dress is tucked in her knickers (social intelligence); we choose to see the bright side of a fairly crappy situation (perspective); we choose to put on our pyjamas and study for an exam when everyone else is putting on their glad rags to go out (self-regulation). Strengths, like any muscle, need to be exercised in order to develop. Without regular application, they get a bit soft and wobbly, which doesn't bode well when it comes to doing regular laps of the decision-making circuit.

According to Seligman's strengths theory (you can read all about it in his book *Authentic Happiness*), each of us possesses 24 strengths (to a greater or lesser degree), which are divided into six overarching categories: wisdom and knowledge; courage; humanity; justice; temperance; and transcendence. Each of these characteristics can be utilised to improve our quality of life and that of others, which we'll explore in a moment. In the meantime, it's time to discover your personal power.

There are a few ways to do this:

- Have a nose through the list on the next page and guesstimate your top three personal strengths. Then, go to AuthenticHappiness.org and take the VIA (Values in Action) Character Strengths survey – a 25-minute exercise (240 questions in total) that ranks your 24 strengths in descending order and compares your answers to thousands of others. A 15-minute user-friendly version of the VIA (Values in Action) Character Strengths survey (120 questions in total) can also be taken on VIACharacter.org.

- Stuck for time? There's also a mini test on Authentic Happiness.org that will give you a bang-on accurate snapshot of where you excel (and your weaknesses to boot). Mystic Megs will love this! Then compare your answers. How does your self-perception stack up to that of the experts?

- Having taken these tests on numerous occasions, I consistently achieve the same results: creativity, perseverance and gratitude. My vitality and zeal, on the other hand, take a beating each time. Just as well I'm not a cheerleader or a motivational speaker. I don't think rallying the troops is my jam.

VIA (Values in Action) Character Strengths (VIACharacter.org)

Wisdom and knowledge – *cognitive strengths*

Creativity, curiosity, judgement, love of learning, perspective

Courage – *emotional strengths*

Bravery, perseverance, honesty, zest

Humanity – *interpersonal strengths*

Love, kindness, social intelligence

Justice – *civic strengths*

Teamwork, fairness, leadership

Temperance – *excess-preventing strengths*

Forgiveness, humility, prudence, self-regulation

Transcendence – *strengths that forge universal connections and meaning*

Appreciation of beauty and excellence, gratitude, hope, humour, spirituality

Once you've identified your strengths (tick that box, List Maker), the rest is simple. Here's how living the good life rolls out:

- Choose work that lets you use these strengths every day.

Not possible? For a lot of us, it isn't. So what's the alternative?

- Recraft your present (career, friends, family, hobbies – you name it) to use your signature strengths more.

That, in fairness, is much more doable. With the help of some conscious-awareness training (coming right up!), the ability to create a present that facilitates our happiness is well within our reach. It does involve turning off our digital devices, though, so why don't you step away from the smartphone, power off that tablet and lock the aul laptop away? We're about to embark on your very own personal strength-training session.

The Great Life: Flow in Action

The good life is a process, not a state of being. It is a direction, not a destination.

CARL ROGERS, *ON BECOMING A PERSON*

Can you remember what you did yesterday? More importantly, can you remember how you felt while you did it? We all like to think of ourselves as special little snowflakes but, in fact, we're kind of predictable. Even if you make a living as a Rasputin impersonator or a freelance sperm-donator, chances are you probably did the same thing yesterday as you did today. Conscious awareness isn't something we put on the top of our 'to do' list, especially when stuck in a traffic jam en route to work at 8.55 am. Our minds get caught up in what's ahead, rather than engaging with what's currently happening, which can make that three-mile tailback feel more like three days. But by applying Seligman's strengths theory to create more flow in our day-to-day doings, we can learn to improve the quality and direction of our attention, thus turning our routines into rituals. What does this have to do with living the good life? Everything.

Flow creates momentum, which has a knock-on effect in all areas of our existence. By shifting our perspective from 'What am I getting out of this?' to 'What am I putting into this?', we create the ideal circumstances for presence – that state of being totally immersed in the moment instead of whiling away the minutes. Start by increasing your satisfaction in minor details and you'll be more likely to take the right turn when it comes to larger life goals. Before long, the good life might well become great. Not a bad deal.

Enough of the small talk. Let's get this show on the road. Notebook and pen at the ready. Using the table on the next page as a guideline, set aside 10 minutes each day from Monday to Sunday to diarise your routine activities. The objective of this exercise is to help convert the daily grind into the daily grand by pinpointing any weak spots that could benefit from some extra flow and using your personal strengths to improve them, to take ordinary tasks and, with some conscious awareness, to make them extraordinary. Here's how it works.

In the interests of timing (and for all of you *Blue Peter* fans), here's one I made earlier from double-sided sticky tape and some pipe cleaners. In fact, it comes straight from a day in the life of my marketing manager friend. Having taken the VIA test, her top strengths are zest, kindness and leadership. The following table represents the low-, mid- and high-flow activities in her day (ranked 1 to 3 – I'll explain this further in a minute), how they make her feel and what strengths can be deployed to improve the quality and direction of her attention.

Let's take a look.

TIME	ACTIVITY	FEELING	FLOW RANK	STRENGTHS	CONVERSION FLOW RANK	CONVERSION FEELING
Early AM 6–9	Gym	Tired	1	Zest	2	Lots of post-workout energy
	Commute to work	Stressed	1	Zest, kindness	1	Still working on this one!
Late AM 9–12	Meetings	Bored to tears	1	Leadership	3	Active participation made it more engaging
	Administration	Unconscious	1	Zest	1	Still working on this one too!
Afternoon 12–2	Mentoring lunch	Helpful but conscious of time pressure	2	Leadership, kindness	3	Committed more to the process by rejigging schedule
Early PM 2–5	Brainstorm session	All over it – tonnes of ideas	3	Teamwork, love of learning	–	–
Late PM 5–9	Dinner with partner	Relaxed, engaged	3	Curiosity, gratitude	–	–
	Cleaning	Noooooooo	1	Zest	2	Like the gym, I felt better once I started

TIME	ACTIVITY	FEELING	FLOW RANK	STRENGTHS	CONVERSION FLOW RANK	CONVERSION FEELING
Night	Take a bath	Relaxed, thankful	3	Gratitude	–	–
9–12	Read a book	Really engaged	3	Love of learning, curiosity	–	–
Core strengths: Zest, kindness, leadership						
Additional strengths: Teamwork, love of learning, curiosity						

You're going to do the exact same. Easy as. Grab your notebook and pen and let's get started.

Activities

Record up to three main activities for each time slot each day. Be honest. If all you did was shower, get dressed and go to work between 6 am and 9 am, that's perfectly fine. If, however, you spent most of your time noodling around on the net, then slot that bad boy in too. Note: don't rank playing Farmville 2: Country Escape as a 3 simply because you lost three hours of your day to playing it when you should've been studying. Flow is challenging, not challenged. We'll get to that in a moment.

Feelings

Jot down how you felt during each activity. Close your eyes and relive the moment if that helps. Dust off that thesaurus. Whatever helps. Just be laser-focused in your clarity. If you wuss out and write 'nice' or 'OK', I may have to hurt you. You've been warned.

Flow rank

Next, assign each activity one of the following flow rankings based on your level of engagement during each one: 1 = no flow; 2 = some flow; 3 = overflowing. Let's start by looking at your lowest-ranking activities, the ones that make you flatline with boredom until there's a small pool of saliva forming under your chin. Anything that coma-inducing tends to be low-flow because the experience is:

- Unrewarding in itself
- Doesn't match our skill sets
- Passive by nature
- A total time-suck.

These often include but are not limited to: household chores, random 'to do' list malingerers (updating car tax or switching bill providers), meetings, administrative tasks like filing (anything from taxes to bits and bobs), decluttering your closet (hey, I'm always available should that be too much for you) and, most of all, the work commute. Nothing like having your nose jammed beneath a stranger's underarm in a glorified cattle cart to set up the day. That said, what one person finds drought-inducing, someone else may consider full-speed flow-mo. Your mission is to increase its potential with a corresponding strength of choice, which brings us to ...

Strengths

Take your top three strengths from the VIA test and apply one to each activity ranked as a 1 or 2 – the ones you are least engaged with. For example, I'd rather sear my eyes out with hot pokers than iron my clothes (aha, the skeleton in *The Happy Closet*!), whereas the prospect of steam and some stiff starch gets my sister hot under the collar every time (there's always one). That being said, when I park my prima-donna tiara and apply perseverance – my top VIA strength – to those creases, I invariably find flow and, by default, answers to any issues I've been mulling over. Keeping present even when your mind wants to check out has its advantages. Studies show that the unconscious mind continues to actively work out problems even while the conscious mind is engaged in a different activity. You should see my hot press after a bout of writer's block. It would put Martha Stewart to shame.

Next, look at your high-flow activities – those you awarded a 3 rating. What do they have in common? As a general rule, the things that grab us in the moment are often shared experiences (anything from a rosemantic dinner for two to a great conversation), something physically or mentally engaging (sport, yoga, gardening, motorcycle maintenance) or something that's total brain fodder (reading, puzzles, playing an instrument or learning a language).

Decide which of the strengths from the 24-strong list best describes each activity. Maybe you riff on a love of learning or get high on gratitude. If so, look at ways in which you can apply these high vibrations to other areas of your life. In recruitment-speak, this is known as a transferable skill (what can I say? Old habits die hard). Perhaps your love of learning can be applied to *listening* to the plumber inform you of what's wrong with the shower rather than nodding and smiling while making mental 'to do' lists. Or perhaps those gratitude guns can bulk up on giving praise for the things you have (even problems can be blessings in disguise) rather than just the things you want.

Conversion

At the end of the week, assess your progress in transforming those ordinary activities into something extraordinary. Did you convert those 1s and 2s to 3s? Has your perspective shifted any? Here's a challenge: try working on some of the additional strengths you discovered in the VIA quiz to stretch yourself even further and improve your core strength base. For example, my friend's collective strength would read something like this:

- Core strengths: Zest, kindness, leadership
- Additional strengths: Teamwork, love of learning, curiosity
- Total strengths: Zest, kindness, leadership, teamwork, love of learning, curiosity

   Is that a satisfaction six-pack I spy?

There you have it: a simple and effective list of your strengths. Know them and deploy them in everything, from the completely absorbing to the utterly mundane, to create flow right here, right now. Not only does it make it life more enjoyable but it can also lead you in the direction of your happy medium. Which reminds me – I never finished my London story. How about we find out more?

Confession Corner

I returned to Dublin from London with no job, nowhere to live and ankle-deep in debt. I had nothing – apart from the letters 'OD' on my bank statement, a few plastic crates of miscellany and a mental file labelled 'life experience' on which to draw. Good times. While my friends were starting families and buying their first homes, I was sofa-surfing, looking for temporary work and starting my life all over again. I could have felt like a failure but instead, I felt relief. Leaving London lifted the burden of my self-imposed expectations from my shoulders.

With absolutely nothing to my name and nothing to show for myself, I had nothing to lose. So I found the reset button, restored those factory settings and spent the guts of a year and a half finding my flow. During that time, I noticed how much happier I was, despite being, in worldly terms, a poster girl for downwards social comparison (see: Argos clothing rail in bedroom, proxy garden furniture in sitting room and a borrowed telly from a mate).

I used my personal strengths – perseverance, gratitude and creativity – to office-temp my way around Dublin while I freelanced as a journalist and grew my contacts list. If I do say so myself, I was a model employee, bar the accounts job where I mistakenly gave pension payments to unsuspecting construction workers. Happy Thursday, guys! I was demoted to the filing cabinet by noon and relieved of my duties by early afternoon.

Despite the payday mishap, I was moving in the direction I wanted to go. I saw small but steady progress and I was surrounded by family and friends. The fact is, I felt like a success. Although my current circumstances looked a bit shabby from the outside (truth be told, my gaff didn't even have curtains), to be honest, I didn't care. After a self-esteem-whipping detour to London, I was back on the right path – the one that pointed me toward my happy medium. I didn't give a curse anymore about who was behind me, in front of me or beside me, how fast or how far they were motoring. I was happy to be pedalling along (no car, remember?) in my own direction, knowing I was right where I should be.

A simple change in my external world – moving back home to Ireland – was enough to redirect my purpose and help me find my flow. Instead of over-scripting the conditions for my *potential* to emerge (and losing the plot), I was now allowing the conditions for my *purpose* to emerge. In layman's terms, I no longer had to try so hard to make it work. Within 18 months, I was freelancing full-time as a writer. Granted, I was still entertaining friends on patio furniture, not exactly that pedalo cocktail bar in the middle of the Arabian Sea, but I truly didn't want anything more. Isn't that the whole point of being happy – wanting what you have? If that's the case, then saying 'thank you' might well be the key to having what you want. Let's find out, shall we?

Gr-attitude: Telling a New Story

The essence of learning to be grateful is to learn to want what you have.

MAUREEN GAFFNEY, *FLOURISHING*

Showing gratitude seems like an easy enough gig. You show up, you say thanks for what you've got, you go about your business. If only it were that simple. It's easy to be grateful when life is tickety-boo but can you throw down the same big love for your share of problems? Exactly! That's when gratitude becomes more than just a good-time sentiment; it becomes an attitude.

A simple shift in perspective is all that's required to give blessings and banes equal billing. With regular practice, you'll soon begin to see how life's balance sheet is tipped in your favour. Consider it a disappointment ointment, an expectation crusher, an entitlement antidote and an envy eradicator. Most of all, consider gratitude a form of presence – on a stick, covered in sticky toffee, just waiting to be enjoyed.

Oprah Winfrey praises the process as 'the quickest, easiest, most powerful way to effect change in your life'. Strong words from one of the most influential women in the world, who, I may add, has reportedly kept a gratitude journal for over 10 years. And we're about to follow her example. You know what that means. It's homework time!

For this exercise, you'll need your trusty notebook and a pen, plus a willingness to see just how good you have it. Our mission? To make gratitude a habit you won't want to kick. As we learned in Chapter 2, the brain loves to be told sweet little lies. So even if you feel like your life has gone to hell in a handbasket, be prepared to praise the smell of singed wicker and the incandescent flames that surround you. We'll get to the 'why' in a moment. List Makers, you're in for a treat. This ought to put your skills to good use. In the meantime, here's a sneak-peak of what you can expect.

- Gratitude is presence – no pining for the future or whining about the past.
- Gratitude slays the green-eyed monster and kills excessive comparison.
- Gratitude improves decision-making by focusing on what matters.

- Gratitude decreases anxiety and worry and gives selfishness the heave-ho.
- Gratitude boosts physical and psychological well-being.
- Gratitude is self-perpetuating. Everyone benefits.
- Gratitude enhances our interpersonal connections.
- Gratitude increases self-esteem.
- Gratitude maximises satisfaction.

By figuring out how to show gratitude for what we have and what we may have wished for in the past but never got, we'll be better positioned to understand why missed opportunities are, with hindsight, the best things we never had. Consider it the universal intelligence at play.

Similar to the feeling the signal exercise in Chapter 3, this is a super-fast fix-it that can be used anywhere, anytime. Much like intuition, gratitude strengthens with practice, leaving you with a sense of immense satisfaction that soon becomes the story you want to tell – your happy medium.

To start off, create a table with four rows, labelled people, possessions, qualities and problems. Divide the fourth row into two columns, past and present – you'll see why. (Check out the table on page 129 for reference.)

People

Who are the MVPs in your crew/clique/fam/gang (delete as appropriate)? Why do they deserve a salute? Don't limit your answer to a good deed someone may have done you, although that's a good start. Go deeper into what it is that keeps them firmly in your sacred squad. A good listener? Makes you laugh? Someone you can rely on? Feel free to go full stream-of-consciousness on this one.

Now try the same process with as many people as you know. The more you realise how important the individuals that surround you are, the more you're likely to match their magnitude. The more you give back, the more you get. And that's no platitude – that's physics, folks. If every action has an equal and opposite reaction as per Newton's Third Law of Motion, then the act of thanks toward another will circle back in the form of feels. All the lovely feels. Oh yeah!

Possessions

Habituation is the brain's biggest enemy. The instant it gets used to something, the less it appreciates it. In *The Happy Closet*, I talked about all the times you 'had to have' a dress or a pair of earrings, only to forget you even had it a few months later. Ring any bells? Scientists call this the hedonic treadmill: where the lifespan of material fulfilment peaks sharply and then evens out once we've adjusted to its presence (about three months). The result? We strive for more in a bid to sustain the high of the initial acquisition. A recent study carried out by scientists at Baylor University highlighted the correlation between high levels of materialism and lower life satisfaction, not to mention increased levels of happiness for those who err on the side of gratitude. That's not to say you shouldn't want those Agent Provocateur suspender briefs, but sending cosmic kudos for what you already have might well be the antidote for that sneaky habit of throwing the glad-eye at every pair of French knickers that you fancy. You see what I mean? That said, a soft spot for the basics never did anyone any harm. My mother, for example, says when she goes to bed at night, she thanks God for a roof over her head, a bed to sleep in and a clear conscience. Now that's something worth having. Mothers – you can't beat 'em!

Qualities

When it comes to personal capital, there are certain assets that often get overlooked. Our pal Aristotle was quick to spot this gap in the market when he introduced us to the Virtues as laid out in *The Nicomachean Ethics*. These are the personal qualities that create character, such as courage, generosity, patience, honesty, friendliness and wittiness, to name a few. Qualities are the strengths (hello, Professor Seligman!) we can use to focus on the good things in our lives and to improve the lot or well-being of others. So you're driving a 16-year old jalopy and most people spend in a week what you earn in a month. You're also a patient, smart, persistent chap with a razor-sharp wit that makes small talk worth the air-time. It's time to think about ourselves differently: these are more than just personal strengths – this is the sum of all good fortune.

Problems

This is where it gets interesting! We're very quick to shake a fist at instead of fist-pumping the universe/God/the source/ ourselves (delete as appropriate) for our life's lot, so this is a golden opportunity to embrace life's more challenging experiences (past or present). A bad break-up? Finances in a jocker? Think about what that problem has taught you. By viewing the predicament from a position of gratitude, you're empowering yourself to learn from troublesome situations in the past, find solutions for the future or at least make peace with the present.

I should know. Cast your mind back to Chapter 3 where I dished the dirt on my own 'problems'. Need a recap? Not on the property ladder, not married, can't drive, of questionable income. What a catch! But on the gratitude flipside, I've also written two books, travelled extensively, have a wonderful family and friends and live in a country I call home. I have oodles of quiet time and a flexible job which allows me the freedom to write. If I had a fleet of kids to worry about and a mortgage to maintain, I may never have had the opportunity to pour all my energies into book writing. I'm a singular-focus kind of gal, so something would have gone by the wayside. That list isn't a consolation prize. It *is* the prize. I want all of these things. In fact, I crave them. Sometimes, life comes gift-wrapped a bit differently to how we expected it. It's up to us to reframe what we have – to focus less on what we consider to be flaws and more on the favours. That said, I still have to get my driver's licence.

Note: the following account contains scenes that have been created for your entertainment.

PEOPLE	My partner, whose patience is rivalled only by that of a sand artist on a windy day.
	My best friend, whose loyalty makes most Labradors look weak.
POSSESSIONS	My velvet ankle boots. When life gets me down, they shout 'get down with your bad self!'
QUALITIES	I'm self-reliant. You could stick me in a shed with a cup of water and I'd have a party.

PROBLEMS	PRESENT	PAST
	Business is slow at the moment but I know from past experience that I have the resilience to see through the rough patches.	Being made redundant was scary but it taught me how to be courageous and inspired me to start my own business.

Review

Now that you've filled out the table, read your story out loud. What is it telling you? There's a lot in your life that's worthy of a hat-tip, a high five or a 'ta muchly'. So your life isn't fairytale-perfect. You're better off. Someone always winds up being locked in a tower, poisoned by an evil stepmother or cursed by a malevolent fairy. And for what? To be permanently indebted to Prince Charming? That's no way to start off a marriage. Just think of all the arguments over who does the housework. 'I saved your life and now you expect me to do the ironing?' Nah. I'll pass, thanks. Thanks a million, actually.

Supersize It!

There's an easy way to supercharge the effects of gratitude. Consider being thankful a bit like a battery juice-pack for your happiness levels – it increases their power, extends their life span and is super convenient too. What if I told you that you could convert positive experiences into lasting changes in your brain? Think about it. If feeling good is the end game (and let's face it, it's the goal behind much of what we do, want and pursue), then just coasting on the feel-good fumes of a positive experience isn't gonna fly. You're going to need more juice if you want to tap into that feeling wellspring for the long haul. According to Rick Hanson, psychologist, author and senior fellow at the Greater Good Science Center at UC Berkeley, there's a little something we can do to imprint positive experiences on the brain in a more conscious manner. He suggests that the way to convert a good experience into something more lasting is by feeling it intensely in the body for as long as possible, then sealing the deal by sensing your intent in feeling the experience sinking in. The trick? Visualisation (more on that in Chapter 6). Use whatever symbolism works for you – a warm feeling, even one of those Snapchat filters with rainbows spilling out of your mouth. Whatever makes it memorable and easy to retrieve should your feel-good storage need replenishing.

OK. So what do we know so far?

- We can't cope with too much choice, let alone limitless choice.
- We're prone to bad decisions when we base outcomes solely on potential.
- We're not great at predicting what will make us happy.
- We've got mad notions.

What did we learn?

- Setting limits helps us contain the experience and keep present.
- Applying our strengths to the present tense creates flow and more satisfaction.
- Saying 'thanks' creates perspective.
- We still have mad notions.

Ah, well. Three out of four ain't so bad. The most important thing about living the good life is learning to set boundaries. Potential is limitless – everyone has it; but not everyone knows how best to deploy it. By establishing boundaries, be they time, attention or money, we put a cap on the options (are you listening, Wheel Spinner?), thereby limiting disappointment and the fear that we are missing out on the rewards enjoyed by others. Boundaries, you might say, help reinforce our happy medium. They also keep out nosey neighbours (more on that in the next chapter). For now, pour yourself a drink, kick back and have a nose in the oh-so-good happiness hacks on the next page.

Happiness Hacks

DECLUTTER YOUR DREAMS

There's a good reason that we are filled with regrets about what might have been and the distracting relics of our unfulfilled goals – because we never gave our story an ending. Don't fall foul of the Zeigarnik effect, a term given by Roy Baumeister and E.J. Masicampo at Florida State University's Department of Psychology to the condition where an unfulfilled goal interferes with the ability to carry out a subsequent task. The takeaway? If you make definite plans to finish one goal rather than setting but not completing numerous ones, your working memory can engage with the present and concentrate on immediate tasks that will allow you to reach your goal, and thus free you from distraction. Remember my lecture on multitasking? I rest my case.

Good for: Frequent Trader, Wheel Spinner

STOP PUSHING SO HARD

Your life is your baby, I know, I know. There's still no excuse for being a pushy pageant mom. This isn't *Toddlers and Tiaras.* As tempting as it is to try to achieve a version of how your life should look, making your kid wear flippers, Dolly Parton wigs and fake tan while twerking to '9 to 5' when she barely knows how to walk might well backfire on you somewhere down the road. Allow your baby to grow with guidance and, most of all, give it some space to surprise you.

Good for: All types

FIND RITUAL IN THE ROUTINE

Our wise friend Confucius believed in bestowing the ordinary with an air of extraordinary by observing daily rituals. Applied to a more modern frame of reference, this can mean anything from setting the table for dinner, applying lippy before leaving the house or always opening the door for somebody. By incorporating a conscious awareness of these seemingly insignificant practices into our daily routine, we not only sanctify the mundane but we also demonstrate our potential to affect change. If God is in the detail, then there's something sacred about life's in-betweens.

Good for: All types

DETACH FROM THE OUTCOME

I'll be happy when I lose 10 pounds. I'll be happy when I get promoted. I'll be happy when hangover-free wine is invented. Ring a bell? We're devils for making our desires conditional on the outcome, which, according to Buddha, is the source of all suffering. Your best bet? Tune into the emotional feedback you hope to get from your goal. What is the feeling you are seeking? Self-esteem? Recognition?

Connection? Your feelings are the signal that tells you where you stand in relation to your happy medium. Tune into this feedback and find excuses to feel these feel-good vibes every day rather than waiting for external circumstances to change. Holding our happiness captive until life pays a handsome ransom doesn't make us happier now. It just makes us more anxious about how long it's going to take until we get paid.

Good for: Eternal Bachelor, Something Better, Neighbourhood Watch

KICK THE BUCKET (LIST)

Life feeling a bit stale? You don't need to BASE-jump off the Burj Khalifa tower or zip-line naked over a crocodile farm to fuel the dopamine in your brain. The easiest way to convert the ordinary into the extraordinary is by committing to small but salient changes – now. Give your seat to a stranger on the bus, try sexting your partner of a Monday (careful with the autocorrect lest 'erotic' becomes 'septic') or take a new route home from work! Give it a go for a few weeks and ask yourself how it feels. As your awareness of the potential for extraordinary experiences around you is raised, your basal ganglia will begin to register this newness as an existing connection. Looking at things with curious eyes allows us an opportunity for creativity and variety, which, in turn, keeps our habits from becoming unconscious or automatic. The result? Instant vitality.

Good for: All types

FORESEE YOUR FUTURE

Pulitzer Prize-winning journalist Charles Duhigg, author of *Smarter Faster Better*, recommends 'building mental models – telling ourselves stories – about what we *expect* to see'. Envisioning what will happen when we undertake certain actions, the potential obstacles along the way and ways of pre-empting them, he maintains, 'makes it easier to decide where your focus should go when your plan encounters real life'. What's more, by considering the multiple outcome scenarios, much like those of the *Choose Your Own Adventures* kids' books, we're exposed to a wider (and sometimes contradictory) set of possibilities, thus empowering us to make more considered choices – provided we keep tabs on our maximising tendencies in the process.

Good for: All types

THE WRITE STUFF

Journaling may appear a tad self-indulgent, but it's got quite the neurological nous. Not only does it improve our perspective on life by reframing challenges but it is known to improve the attention span of the working memory, which, as we've discovered, has a limited capacity management.

Basically, if there's no room at the inn, journaling can help give those memories a bed for the night until they can be rehomed. In short: we remember more; we remember better.

Good for: All types

BE TIME-SAVVY

Nobel Prize-winning psychologist Daniel Kahneman (notable for his work on decision-making) believes the one variable that people can change in relation to their happiness levels is the allocation of their time. The man's got a point. Time is often treated as something that happens to us rather than something we can allocate. His recommendation? Tilt the balance toward more feel-good activities like making time for friends and, where possible, reduce the dreaded work commute. Take a tandem bike to the office, perhaps?

Good for: All types

EXPECT LESS

No, this isn't a slacker anthem. Lowering your expectations slightly can greatly increase your chances of satisfaction. Maureen Gaffney, author of *Flourishing*, suggests selecting social norms that allocate your unconscious attention to sensible expectations of yourself. In other words, don't expect to be the opening act for Celine Dion's Vegas residency if you've only been asked to sing at closing time in pubs. Selecting goals that mirror your talents goes a long way to staving off the spectre of excessive comparison.

Good for: All types

CHAPTER 6

JOMO: Turning Fear into Joy

The Joy of Missing Out

How much I missed, simply because I was afraid of missing it.

PAULO COELHO, *BRIDA*

There's a story I love to tell about my mother, who, in a bid to avoid an unannounced visitor, hid in the front closet of our house and had my sister answer the door. The interloper, who somehow managed to invite herself in, stood chatting in dangerous proximity to my mother's not-so-secret hiding place. As Mrs O puffed away on her lit cigarette while drinking a cup of coffee (in the dark), my sister caught sight of a thin trail of smoke escaping from the wood shutters. To her credit, she somehow managed to shimmy the guest outside, away from the incriminating evidence, before the faint odour of menthol could give the game away. 'I just couldn't face company,' admitted my mother, almost pleadingly, while still sitting in the closet, still smoking and rather happy, truth be told.

Who could blame her? Sometimes we all want to hide from the world, especially with the incessant demands on our time these days. It can be exhausting trying to be all things to all people (some of whom we don't even like) when all we want to do is find our own closet in which to have a quiet ciggie and a hot scald.

Fear of unwanted social interaction notwithstanding, the fear of missing out (otherwise known as FOMO) can be an equally difficult anxiety to shift. No one likes being left in the shade, although some do choose to smoke in the dark! It's just not in our DNA. Community bonding underpins our most basic human instincts, a fact that has been cleverly tapped into by our permanently-connected, socially-networked culture. Prehistoric physical threats (being pursued by a wildebeest) have evolved into equally acute emotional fears about perceived social exclusion (the equivalent of becoming a wildebeest treat), which keeps us primed and online at all times. Thought Netflix and chill was a good idea last night, did you? Not anymore. Just look at everyone having fun – without you. Ah, diddums. Is that regret I smell?

A bit of background: the term FOMO (fear of missing out) was first coined in 2011 by entrepreneur and investor Caterina Fake in a blog post entitled 'FOMO and Social Media'. According to Fake, the online platforms and social networks that we've all come to love both create and cure FOMO. In other words, scrolling through feeds may reinforce the feeling that we're missing out but, by the same token, they also give us to a sense that we're participating, even when we're not.

So essentially you *are* at that invite-only London Fashion Week party, even if you're actually sitting alone in your studio flat watching *Frasier* reruns, feeling like Billy No Mates. Need I remind you that you didn't want to go in the first place? And that you were quite happily drinking a cold beer and eating pizza in your fuzzy slippers before being summoned by the tablet of trepidation to see what you traded off on? Champagne, sushi and oysters? Goody bags from Net-a-Porter? Hanging out with David Gandy? WHHHHHHHHHY?

Why, indeed. Our attachment to FOMO is a sticky wicket of a habit but one not beyond cutting loose, provided we're prepared to shift our perspective, swap a consonant and reframe missed opportunities as deliberate decisions. It's time to turn FOMO (fear of missing out) into JOMO (joy of missing out). Just ask Anil Dash, writer, activist and friend of Caterina Fake, who upped the acronym ante in 2012 on his blog with a post called 'JOMO!' that celebrated the emotional agency of periodic unplugging to reconnect with what really matters. By putting more 'free' in our time, we can balance our online and offline lives, eliminate regret and allow satisfaction to crowd out the meaningless soundbites that wreck our heads. In short,

JOMO allows for mindfulness, freedom and space to think. You don't know what you're missing out on – and you don't want to either. Sounds like a happy medium to me.

A bit like my mother, we all need to press Ctrl-Alt-Delete every once in a while so that we can reboot our system. We took our first tentative steps in creating a happy balance with the digital detox in Chapter 2. Now we're going to look at how we can establish boundaries to increase the peace and protect our quality time so that JOMO becomes second nature. No more trading off on life's sweet small moments. The buck stops here. And it all starts with a well-placed 'no'.

JOMO	FOMO
Present tense	Future tense
Joy	Anxiety
Personal agency	No agency
Deliberate decision	Second-guessing choice
Rewards enjoyed by you	Rewards enjoyed by others
Exclusive	Excluded
Time-out	Time-suck

The 'No'-Fly Zone

Make 'no' a complete sentence.

AMY POEHLER, *YES PLEASE*

As chief bottle-washer of your own well-being, it's your responsibility to establish a personal 'no'-fly zone – a clear, unified operations procedure that enforces your happy medium. Consider it a satisfaction safeguard to limit FOMO and protect your precious time from unwanted distractions. If someone flies over your airspace, feel free to let a 'no' fly and hit them square in the kisser. Trust me, it's very therapeutic. Let's get cracking then.

On the next few pages are two tried-and-tested methods of transitioning from FOMO to JOMO without feeling like a social outcast/selfish parent/bad friend (delete as appropriate). There are two manoeuvres: the interruption audit and the 'me' timer. In an ideal world, we'd perform the interruption audit before any situation that taps into that deep-seated Darwinian death threat (remember Chicken Little?). Just for the record: time and space won't collapse because you couldn't attend your next-door neighbour's niece's communion. It'll be grand, honestly. In that ideal world, we'd also make a daily practice of the 'me' timer – a short and sweet sabbatical that'll keep time on your side, whatever tries getting in the way.

To avoid perpetual airspace infringement, you must be crystal clear on your procedure objectives, as wiggle room is often misinterpreted as weakness. Furthermore, the effectiveness of your 'no'-fly zone is dependent on regional support, so ensure you have a wingman (a bit like my sister) who can implement this policy should someone try overstepping your boundaries if, like my mother, you should be sequestered in a cupboard or other holding area.

Ironically, in turning something down, we disappoint fewer people – and, most importantly, we don't disappoint ourselves. It's what separates a job well done from several jobs undone. Unless you're privy to some sort of cloning device that'll help you run a half-marathon, bake four dozen iced fairy cakes for charity, help the new guy in work move house, attend your best friend's surprise birthday bash and somehow make it to that Rolling Stones concert (corporate box seats!) all on the same day, chances are something's gotta give. Establishing stronger boundaries on how we use our time frees us up to concentrate on what's most important. By becoming more deliberate about what you expect from your daily schedule, you're better positioned to make easier decisions about how to use it and manage any lingering FOMO. It's up to you to decide what makes the cut. How about we find out?

The Interruption Audit

We've seen how interruptions can scatter our attention, upend our focus and hang our happy medium out to dry. We've also seen how limiting our options facilitates ease and allows us to make smarter choices. The more limitations we put on choice, the less confusion we face, the less stress we experience and the more our creativity can flourish. Possibilities expand as life slows down – not the other way around. By choosing deliberately and mindfully, we begin to understand the *why* behind our decisions and, in turn, find more purpose, direction and meaning.

In *The Happy Closet*, I introduced readers to the 'to don't' list – an exercise designed to help shoppers commit to what they wouldn't wear as opposed to what they would. This beautifully backward logic helps break bad habits and build new identity-based behaviours. In other words, discovering what you don't want flips the script from self-denial to self-empowerment. Apply the same principle to your 'no'-fly zone with the help of the interruption audit and FOMO becomes JOMO in a heartbeat. Nice one.

Need some pointers? Here's how to turn a 'to do' into a 'to don't'. When faced with an event you feel you need to attend or something you're under pressure to do, grab your trusty notebook and pen and ask yourself the following questions:

- What am I being asked to do?

- Why should I do it?
- Why shouldn't I do it? (Didn't think you were getting off the hook that lightly, did you?)
- Who benefits?
- What suffers?
- How do I feel about it?

Let's put this into context. Say, for instance, you've been invited to a work mixer that oozes with networking potential. Getting face-time with the big guys could mean a possible promotion down the road. Best start planting those seeds now, eh? But wait! Didn't your doctor insist you take extra rest this week on account of that nasty case of shingles you recently acquired? You might be itching for a title upgrade (boom cha!), but you've got to look at the bigger picture, my friend. Besides, trying to figure out how to have a sneaky scratch while the VP of marketing riffs about the latest campaign strategy may not be the golden opportunity you imagined. To do? Not so much.

When writing *The Happy Medium,* for example, I put JOMO at the top of my priority list by enforcing the following limits: I scaled back on my work commitments as far as I could financially sustain for a three-month period, then I activated my out of office for three months which read something like this:

I'm taking some time out to write my second book so apologies if I don't respond to your mail. You may contact me on the number below if your query is urgent; otherwise, I'll catch up with you all in mid-July. Thanks for your understanding.

I did the same with my social media accounts and put myself on social hiatus while I finished writing the book. The prospect of missing out on meeting friends and attending work events was mitigated by the bigger picture – submitting my manuscript within a set timeframe. Those three months became my 'no'-fly zone. The great thing about it? By explaining my rationale to friends and family, I could fall off the grid without falling out of favour. Everyone was entirely supportive of the whole process, offering to help in any way they could. Had I assumed otherwise and overextended myself, things could have turned out very differently.

If in doubt, remember: there's always a FOMO trade-off. Sometimes, we have to exchange kicks and giggles for eight hours' consecutive shut-eye so that we can deliver a presentation the next day without feeling like we've been dragged through a hedge backward. And other times, we've got to take one for the team and do a solid for someone in need. Life always presents us with ebb and flow. It's up to us to establish the checks and balances as we figure out our happy medium. Consider the checklist above a handy tool, one for the back pocket when overwhelm comes knocking and perspective has made a run for the door.

The 'Me' Timer

When it comes to 'me' time, we tend to get sandblasted with an abrasive case of the guilts. Call it conditioning, call it societal pressure, call it whatever you want; there's no glossing over the fact that we're all prone to confusing self-care with selfishness. Taking 20 minutes to sit in your garden? Slacker! Swapping that optional after-work function for a much-needed yoga class? Part-timer!

It's not that we want to be *that* busy, but not wanting to can carry a larger stigma: not being a team player, not caring or, worse, not being hungry enough. Toss in the fear of job loss or social exclusion and the result is, literally, overwhelming. Anxiety, burnout and stress can all combine to have a pernicious effect on our lives – so it's time to establish small but regular personal boundaries in a bid to maintain our happy medium.

The beauty of the 'me' timer exercise is its short and sweet disposition: it carves out a pocket of time dedicated to you and you only that can mean the difference between feeling frazzled and feeling focused, thriving or barely surviving. Consider this your daily 'no'-fly zone. Should anyone interrupt this sacred session, you've got permission to shoot them down with a steely stare. The idea is to create space in your routine for ritual and gain a sense of agency in your day.

For this exercise, you'll need:

- A timer
- Time.

Begin by deciding how much time you have to allocate to yourself. If your diary is heaving like a Balmain sample sale, start small. Try setting aside 10 minutes every day for a month dedicated to your well-being. How you fill your 'me' time is entirely up to you. Ideally, it should be something that feeds flow on which you can surf the rest of your day. Come the second month, increase that number to 15 or 20 minutes and see how you feel.

Once you start reaping the benefits of your practice, you'll begin to get clarity on the things that matter and those that don't. If you have one of those days that hits you over the head and you have no choice but to do everything, this ritual will reinforce a sense of control in an otherwise chaotic world. Set your timer. Your time starts now!

For me, my 'me' timer starts at 7 am every morning for a half hour. I'm a sucker for a French press and the radio and those 30 minutes before giving myself over to the day. Why? Because there's no compelling reason to accomplish anything bar enjoying that alone time with a cup of coffee, some easy listening and my thoughts. What motivates me upon waking is that quiet corner of time; what comes afterwards is a consequence of that.

My friend takes a book into the bathroom and reads for 10 minutes while her husband keeps their toddler occupied. Little Johnny knows if Mommy is 'taking a bath', he can't barge in, so she cleverly co-opts this knowledge to her advantage when in need of a mini reboot. Needless to say, Johnny is going to grow up thinking adults bathe several times a day. Meh! A small price to pay.

Now that we've limited FOMO with some mindful diary management, our task is to fill those gaps of time by increasing JOMO. Meditation creates JOMO by helping us focus on and connect with the moment. Scientific studies support claims that the practice of meditation reduces stress and anxiety by taking the brainwaves into an alpha state, which helps us not to feel overwhelmed.

Think of it like expandable foam: something that insulates against life's little speed wobbles and reinforces our happy medium. For me, I like to finish my day with 10 minutes of meditation and a mental gratitude riff on what I've got to be thankful for. This keeps me tapped into the present and less likely to ruminate on what I did or didn't do that day, how things played out or what I could have done differently. It stops my inner maximiser from keeping me awake at night and quietens the Miss Moan who has a habit of b*tching and whining when she doesn't get her way.

When it comes to mind games, some are definitely worth playing. Let's check 'em out.

How to Meditate Without Losing Your Mind

If you want to conquer the anxiety of life, live in the moment, live in the breath.

AMIT RAY, *OM CHANTING AND MEDITATION*

You are about to embark on a meditative journey. Shortly, you will be guided into a state of deep relaxation. Expect to feel full-body awareness and clear, judgement-free thoughts. Allow yourself to be fully present in the moment as you connect your inner world of thought and feeling with the breath. Breathe in. Breathe out. You are aware of nothing but awareness itself. Feel this awareness with every breath. In and out. Out and in. Your body is completely relaxed. Your mind is completely aware. Start to notice the thoughts that come up. Don't think about them too much. Just notice them as they pass by. *What's that? They're not leaving?* Don't judge. Don't engage. Just allow them to drift away in their own time. *Sorry, they're throwing things at you? And shouting?* Well, use this as an opportunity to practice non-attachment. Acknowledge but don't identify the content of your thoughts, just ... *Sorry, what's that? They're jumping up and down and refusing to leave?* Right, then. Continue to breathe deeply as I guide your attention to a big fluffy cloud. It's floating right above your head. This is your safe place. What does your cloud look like? *Black? And menacing? Really? Work with me here.* Try experiencing the calming effects of these restful settings instead: an ocean. A deep, blue ocean. A beach. A long, sandy beach. A breeze. A cool, calm breeze. A candle. *A burning candle.* A burning candle? *No, seriously. I smell burning. Is that the curtains? Oh, sh*t!*

Ah, meditation. We'd all be masters of Zen-like calm if only we weren't so damn distracted. *Sorry, where was I ...* Besides, who has the time to sit lotus-style and chant 'om'? Surely that whole malarky is for people who eat mung bean salad and read Eckhart Tolle, not for normal folk. Wrong. Oh, how very wrong. Meditation is more than an esoteric exercise for the spiritually-inclined. It's the singularly most effective tool in clearing distractions and helping us make better decisions – which, as we've discovered by now, is central in our journey to a happy medium. Allow me to sell it to you.

Meditation 101

The aim of meditation is to retrain our attention by observing the patterns and habits of the mind. Styles range from spiritual to practical, active to passive, breath-based to mantra-focused, all with similar results – improved concentration, mental clarity and emotional acuity. In other words, all the crap that once seemed important quickly loses its cache when you meditate, leaving you free to cultivate new ways of looking at the world.

Meditation also makes us better people. Arianna Huffington, co-founder and former editor-in-chief of the Huffington Post Media Group and author of *Thrive*, maintains that apart from helping us connect with ourselves, it also 'increases our ability to connect with others, actually making us more compassionate'. If connection is one of the cornerstones of lasting happiness, then prepare for a feel-good future. We'll be going deeper into that topic in Chapter 7.

And wait, there's more. Meditation is a next-level ninja when it comes to the attention–distraction conundrum. According to a study carried out by Harvard researchers, meditation helps develop the mind's plasticity and its attendant ability to bounce back more quickly from a distraction.

Quick neuroscience 101: plasticity refers to the brain's ability to redecorate the gaff in a bid to tune into your needs. In other words, the mind can reorganise its living space by creating new neural pathways when required. As we know, all it takes is a ping, a ring or similar audible alert to hijack our conscious awareness. Meditative practice helps us guide back our thoughts to the task at hand when summarily interrupted.

Remember the basal ganglia? How could you forget? Her penchant for automated processes and streamlining the brain's workload, as we know, is a double-edged sword – laudable when mastering a good habit, less so when committing our compulsions to muscle memory. But meditation can help change our habitual mental patterns, not to mention repetitive thoughts – the intrusive ones that scream and shout and won't go away. What's more, it's also a formidable form of mental self-regulation, which over time becomes an automatic habit in itself. Bye-bye, niggly worries; hello, mental clarity.

I should know. I've been practising meditation for about four years now. Prior to starting, I was an unofficial ambassador for low-level anxiety. I had six crowns put on my teeth due to a chronic case of stress-induced bruxism. I had hospital EKG tests for heart palpitations (also stress-induced) and I'd frequently find myself wide awake at night with insomnia (also stress-induced). And those were just the physical ailments. Don't get me started on the ruminating thoughts and mental chatter. My head felt like Grafton Street during a power cut on Christmas Eve just before shops close. Pure chaos.

My initial attempts at meditation met with limited success, in part because my perception of what meditation should be (wafting incense, contemplating the meaning of life) got in the way of what was actually happening (wandering mind, wondering if I left the immersion on). The reality of sitting with your thoughts – whether pedestrian or frenetic – and just observing them can feel frustrating and pointless. Give it time, however, and the results are pretty impressive. Don't take it from me. Why don't you make your own mind up?

Meditation Styles

Meditation is like a mind-gym, equipped with various machines according to your tastes and skill level. There's no point diving head-first into the full Tibetan Buddhist experience if your idea of concentration is spending 10 minutes watching telly without texting. Then again, if you're not the touchy-feely type, perhaps skip the loving-kindness style and opt for a more cerebral body scan technique? I've done the honours of composing a 'best of' compilation below. Choose your favourite and we'll get cracking on a crash course in a few – just you and me.

The **body scan technique** is a boon for sofa spuds, lazy bones and anyone who spends too much time in their head. Lying flat on the ground, limbs akimbo, the aim of this practice is to create focused attention by alternating between a wide and narrow focus – ranging from each of your 10 little piggies through to the top of your head. Train your inner maximiser to experience how it feels rather than how the feeling can be changed. Oh, and bring some tissues. This one is known for opening up the floodgates and releasing all the feels!

Effortless presence has more of a 'go with the flow' appeal so it's perfect for stress bunnies and the permanently distracted. Here's how it works. Unlike practices that rely on a specific focal point (object, sound, breath), this style (also referred to as 'non-meditation') allows whatever arises in the moment to be the object of your attention. Feeling distracted? Good! Why?

Because that distraction is now your focal point. The idea is to reframe interruptions as intentions rather than constantly bringing the mind back to the breath. This open-door distraction policy helps eradicate self-judgement and redirects us to the task at hand.

Loving-kindness does what it says on the tin. By focusing on 'metta', or love without attachment, this practice aims to cultivate compassion and goodwill toward others. The big sell? Consistent practice stimulates the insula – the brain's happiness centre – and improves your mood. Start by sending laser beams of unconditional love toward yourself (not always the easiest thing to do); then target friends, strangers and enemies alike until you reach a cosmic critical mass. Think good vibrations all the way!

Mantra meditation (OM) riffs on repetition. By focusing the mind on a repeated sound or word, this practice aims to increase attention and ease mental chatter. Looking for the full mala bead experience? Use a mantra. Mantras can be assigned by a spiritual teacher but the option is there to choose one of your own accord. If reciting 'cheeseburgers' relaxes a cognitive clench, then repeat your Big Mac mantra silently the allocated number of times. Feeling your mind wander? Standard. Just guide it back and keep going.

Mindfulness meditation boasts buzzworthy status, not least due to its reputation for knocking anxiety square in the chops. Also referred to as MBSR (mindfulness-based stress reduction), its practical application (and scientific back-up) makes it an attractive alternative for spiritually-disinclined. So what's the gig? 1. Breathe. 2. Focus on the present moment – warts and all; whatever comes up, make like Teflon and let it slide. 3. Distracted? Kick judgement to the curb and redirect your attention back to the present. 4. Repeat.

Taoist meditation brings a brain buffet of styles to the meditation mat. Looking to improve concentration? Why not try a *Zhuanqi* breathing meditation? Mind all a jumble? Declutter with an emptiness meditation. More of a visual soul? Perfect your inner vision with *Neiguan*. Whatever your jam, the common aim is to become one with the *Tao* by connecting body, mind and spirit. Novices may want to take a rain-check on this one.

Third-eye meditation (a.k.a. *trataka*) may sound like hippie hokum, but its results are less woo-woo, more *wu wei*. By focusing your vision (also known as 'gazing') and visualising the colour purple on the space between your eyebrows in the middle of your forehead (known scientifically as the pineal gland), it amplifies intuition, balances both sides of the brain and thus helps you make more considered decisions. The result? Less mental chatter, more clearheaded and a free gift with every practice – added compassion. Not a bad deal.

Transcendental meditation is the uncrowned celebrity of meditation techniques. Known to its fans as TM, its effortless style gained popularity in the '70s by the Beatles and the Beach

Boys. Popular, perhaps; populist, not so much. Adherents pay a nice chunk of change to be assigned a bespoke mantra and a licensed technique by a guru. That said, it is credited with a host of results from improved academic performance to decreased blood pressure and increased alpha waves in the prefrontal cortex – the seat of your brain's executive judgement – which encourages relaxation and feel-good feels.

Vipassana meditation (meaning 'insight' in Sanskrit) gets the democratic thumbs-up. Credited as the oldest form of Buddhist meditation, it's a firm favourite with newbies and veteran practitioners alike. The science bit? Its practice encourages intuitive changes to take place in the grey matter, leading to increased internal awareness. What's more, it's a proven stress-buster. Boom! Beginners start with noticing the breath without judgement and over time can progress to the 'contemplation of reality' stage, should that be your cup of green tea. The benefits? Studies show that three months' immersion training can sharpen the brain enough to help notice otherwise overlooked details. Sayonara, inattentional blindness!

Zazen meditation (a.k.a. Zen) is the Yoda of meditation practices. It's a simple, seated style (there's a walking one too): practitioners work on having a straight body with soft muscles and 'thinking about not thinking'. Piece of cake, right? By focusing on the breath, the aim is to observe thoughts, feelings, and sensations but never to identify with them, however distracting. To make things interesting, Zen masters administer *kōans*, or intuitive-based riddles, to their students for the purpose of contemplation (and insight) during their practice. In the words of everyone's favourite Jedi Master, 'Try not. Do … or do not. There is no try.' In other words, detach from the outcome. Just be. Not do.

Meditation Made Simple

When it comes to meditation, it's best to adapt the 'easy does it' principle. Start with the basics, continue with the basics and advance to the basics. You don't need sacred elephant incense sticks infused with bdellium resin, a cosmic buckwheat hull-filled cushion or sitar music containing subliminal blessings to get you into the right mindset. You just need a window of time in which to marshal your attention. Everything else is just window-dressing. Time's a-wasting. How about some basic training then?

The Setting

Firstly, organise some quiet time. Ten minutes daily is all you'll need. For some, finding 10 spare minutes is as likely as spotting a unicorn having a pint down your local – mythical and with good reason. Kids, jobs, urban soundtracks (see: ambulances, shouty people, drunk people, neighbours doing DIY at random hours) and the daily grind often conspire to ensure our life is lived at over 100 decibels, which is why it is crucial that you find the time to clear your mind. If that means locking yourself in the bathroom/shed/attic/storage cupboard (delete as appropriate) for a piece of peace, then do it. You've got my permission. Whatever setting you find, ensure the place is relatively clutter-free. Meditation can be tricky enough without having to deal with competing distractions like piles of dirty underwear, stacks of bills and unwashed dishes that, like curious zoo creatures, have a unique way of commanding our interest.

The Dress Code

Make sure you're wearing loose, comfortable clothing. Trust me. If you're going to sit in one spot for any length of time, you can't be distracted by a muffin top making a bid for freedom over the waistband of your skinny jeans or having to release a trapped boob from the grips of an underwire bra while 'thinking about not thinking'. What works best are tracksuits, pyjamas, loungewear – anything that functions like extras in a movie: present but not so much that they throw shapes at the camera in a bid to steal the show.

The Posture

Next, you'll need either a chair or a pillow on which to place your posterior. If you're sitting in a chair, keep your chin up, back straight and legs bent at the knees, upon which you'll place your hands. Pillow practitioners, take to the floor. Sit in any of the styles below with your chin up, back straight and arms resting with palms up on your knees.

- Quarter-lotus: Legs crossed with both feet below the opposite thigh or knee
- Semi-lotus: Left foot resting on the opposite thigh with right leg tucked under
- Full lotus: Each foot resting on the opposite thigh
- Burmese: Legs crossed with both knees and tops of feet resting on the floor
- Seiza: Kneeling (use a pillow or blanket as a prop between your bottom and calves)

A few helpful caveats: avoid sitting on the bed. You'll only be tempted to take a cheeky nap. The object here is conscious awareness, not semi-conscious slumber with a side of pillow drool. Also, don't close your eyes completely. This will only induce said state of semi-conscious slumber. Instead, keep your eyes soft with the lids partially closed. This keeps the retinae from taking a sneaky peek at the curious zoo creatures surrounding you and making plans to tidy them all up when your mind should be focused on the present moment. Out of sight, out of mind.

Now that we've cleared that up, you're all set to meditate. Now what? Glad you asked. I'm going to let you in on my own mindfulness meditation practice – a mix of ancient practices and my own imagination. Unconventional? Maybe. Effective? I like to think so. Let's get cracking.

The Technique

Start by taking a few deep breaths – in through the nose and out through the mouth. Give it welly. Really let it rip on the exhale and get rid of all the stale air and stale experiences from the day. Do this a few times before returning to your normal breath. Then, continue to gently follow the natural rhythm of your breath. Nothing fancy; just observe it.

Any nasal breathers or *Star Wars* fans out there? Play to your strengths and try the *Ujjayi* breath (pronounced 'oojai') – an ancient yogic technique that also serves to calm both mind and body. Simply seal your lips and breathe in deeply through the nose and out slowly through the nose while tightening the muscles in the back of your throat. The guttural sound is said to mimic that of the ocean, although you'll probably find it sounds more like Darth Vader. Apologies if that's all you can think of now. Consider it your first lesson in effortless presence. The evil Galactic Empire emissary is now part of your practice. Who'd have thought?

Visualisation

This is where it gets interesting. Visualisation meditation enhances self-awareness and focuses the mind. If you've had a heavy week on the internet, this is the jobby for you. Not only does it have the potential to clear the digital exhaust from our mental atmosphere, it can relieve stress too. Consider it a form of disciplined daydreaming, which brings me to my next point. Resist the temptation to shut your eyes. It may feel easier to meditate this way, but Sleepy Town doesn't need another resident. If you can daydream with your eyes wide open, then you can visualise while meditating with your eyes partially shut.

Now for the fun part: putting visualisation into practice. Are you ready? Imagine a warm summer's day. You're nestling deep into a deck-chair overlooking a garden in full bloom. In your hand is a glass of fresh orange juice/beer/lemonade (delete as appropriate). Your breath is sitting beside you in another chair (yes, your breath. Work with me on this one). This is the first piece of quality time you and your breath have had together all day. Let's face it: if we take anything for granted, it's got to be our breath. Considering it keeps you alive, five to ten minutes of daily one-on-one time is a small ask. Consider this an opportunity to hear what it has to say. Pay attention to its ins and outs. What does it sound like? Is it hushed and delicate? Does it delve deep into your belly with a sonorous sweep? Perhaps it feels trapped somewhere between your breastbone and throat. Allow it to communicate how it feels, being mindful of its message, without trying to 'fix' it. Just allow it to offload.

Happy to be spending time together, continue listening to your breath while your thoughts play together on the grass in front of you. Like a bunch of overexcited kids, they will run about – some are loud, others quiet; some repeatedly vie for your attention. Observe them with an air of non-attachment from the comfort of your chair. They're just playing – there is no need to interfere, control or scold them. Naturally, some thoughts begin to wander out of sight. When they do, guide them back to the grass and continue your time with your breath. Don't be distracted by the distraction. Just let it pass. Never get angry or frustrated with your thoughts, however intrusive. They are just playing, after all. Instead, focus on the sensation of you and your breath enjoying this time together.

One reason our minds wander like curious toddlers is that we believe the 'story' of our thoughts. In other words, we get sucked into the emotionally-charged soap opera of the past and the future, rather than making like a zebra crossing and allowing our thoughts to move along. Keen on breaking free of old dramas that keep repeating themselves? Then just label your thoughts as 'thoughts', rather than 'good thoughts' or 'bad thoughts'. The more you do this, the sooner they'll stop distracting you from your happy medium.

Insider tip: for me, visualising my thoughts as children makes me calmer when they act up or interrupt my breath work. If that doesn't work for you, try visualising your thoughts taking place on a screen in front of you – like when the television is playing while you're doing housework. By externalising thoughts in this way, they gradually become unobtrusive background noise. Whether a bunch of kids at play or *The Real Housewives of Orange County*, the idea is to be aware of your thoughts but not to engage with them.

Some might say that I've been sniffling the aul incense but, hey, it works for me. I get quality time with my breath, which I summarily ignore in the course of a day unless, of course, I'm panting like a basset hound in heat after attempting to run up the stairs (never a good idea). The idea is to find what works for you. To help you on your path, I'm doling out some extra meditation munchies – perfect snack-sized practices for on-the-go. No excuses. Trust me; your happy medium will thank you for it.

Putting the App in Happy

For those of you who still maintain you don't have the time to meditate, I'm here to call major shenanigans. Now that you're not maniacally scrolling through Facebook to see what you're missing, you've got a window in which to schedule some solitude. Ha, busted! Think of it this way: all it takes is up to 10 minutes a day to slow down and recharge. No sagebrush, no singing bowls, no vision quest; just a few pro user tools to help lower stress and bring balance to your life. Do you have 600 seconds to spare?

Headspace is the Dalai Lama of meditation apps: user-friendly, unthreatening and easy-to-understand. That would explain its increasing popularity – 6 million users and counting. Enter Bristol-born former Buddhist monk Andy Puddicombe who co-founded Headspace in a bid to demystify meditation and make it relevant to the masses. Puddicombe's dedication to making meditation accessible to people with modern lives is hinged on his belief that all it takes is 10 minutes a day using proven techniques to be happier and have a bit more clarity. Expect a series of Take 10 guided meditations with Andy, who leads you through easy-to-follow meditation techniques in his inimitable voice. Each Take 10 day builds on the next, reinforcing the technique until it becomes second nature. Meditation reminders aid accountability, as does the app's buddy system. Upgrade your subscription for packages that deepen your practice or themed packs for improving health, relationships and performance. Best suited to newbies, kids, the time-strapped and the curious but cautious. Prepare to be converted.

Buddhify puts the speaker in bespoke with over 80 custom guided mindfulness meditation tracks voiced by six different instructors. It's designed for real-time lives and day-to-day stresses – being online, waiting around, insomnia, dealing with difficult emotions. Tracks range from four to 27 minutes, with a solo meditation timer should you wish to go it alone. The little-and-often school of thought is easier to maintain as a habit than sitting under a bodhi tree for seven days like Buddha. Measurement tools such as progress stats and a check-in system help with accountability and motivation. List Makers will love the pie chart used to track progress, including record streaks and minutes spent meditating. There's also a community FAQ (is it normal to fall asleep? Why do I keep thinking of laundry?) of all those questions you were afraid to ask but are so glad someone else did! It also offers over 100 tips on maximising your mindfulness practice. Perfect for Frequent Traders, Eternal Bachelors and List Makers, for busy people and for times when a helpful distraction is needed (rebooting a computer, waiting for a delayed flight or walking down a crowded city street).

Jiyo is a well-being companion that vows to be 'your better half'. It's also the brainchild of Deepak Chopra – best-selling author, alternative medicine practitioner and de facto mindfulness guru, not to mention a close personal friend of Oprah Winfrey. His aim? To get one billion people actively working toward self-improvement with the help of what he terms 'purposeful technology'. This is the fella who heads up the popular Chopra Center in California, where more than three million people have taken mind, body, spirit classes. Expect video content from Chopra and other experts across topics from meditation and yoga to nutrition and tackling issues like body awareness, stress and self-reflection. Its community functionality means members benefit from mutual support in pursuit of their wellness goals. The app connects to your FitBit, iPhone Health app or Apple Watch so it can personalise health suggestions according to your sleep, exercise and stress habits. It can also help you find nearby exercise and yoga studios. Yep, Big Brother is watching you – but it's all for the greater good.

Whil taps into our culture's fixation with curation and customisation. Boasting over 1,250 yoga and meditation recordings from thought leaders and mindfulness consultants, this app allows users to build a library of tracks tailored to suit every mood and situation. Think of it as Spotify for the mind. The entry-level Mindfulness 101 features introduction meditations in as little as one minute across different categories like health, work and sleep. Overwhelmed by the options? The WhilPower™ search tool features specific sessions, from learning to harness the brain's natural antidepressant power to mindfulness at work and how to become a sleep ninja. Choose how you're feeling at that moment (anxious, grateful, insecure), then set your intention (quiet your inner critic, be happier, overcome fear) and how much time you have to get a recommended session for your needs. And if that's not enough, there's also a library for teens and one for budding leaders. Perfect for Frequent Traders, Eternal Bachelors and Mystic Megs.

Meditation Studio makes a solid argument for its nominal download fee: it's less than the price of a nice coffee, plus it's open 24/7 and allows puppies. Not bad. That's the thing about this app: it's all about taking the complication out of a practice that aims to be uncomplicated. It doesn't hurt that their team of top-brass wellness experts range from Zen Buddhist monks to clinical psychologists. Meditation dilettantes are guided toward a 15-day intro course of bitesize lessons that'll take you from zero to Zen in no time; while serious punters can opt for a deeper immersion with more in-depth sessions. In the same vein as Whil, Meditation Studio allows users to build their own personal libraries from collections entitled 'Be Happy', 'Be Awesome', 'Be Curious', 'Be Kind' and 'Be Healthy'. With over 200 guided meditations featuring different instructors and styles, it sounds like a recipe for option paralysis, but the navigation is intuitive and easy-to-use. Plus the app looks swanky-pants on a retina display!

So how did it go? With your mental decks cleared and 10 minutes of total silence on your side, you should be feeling cooler, calmer and more collected. Some of you may have received some flash insights (a bit like my ironing scenario) as if from nowhere, while some of you might still be wondering how this whole sitting and breathing schtick works. Fear not.

Practice is key to tapping into our internal WiFi signal – the wisdom, intuition, feelings and instinct that keep us in range of our happy medium. If we don't tune into the signal, we'll never turn in the right direction. Once we've plugged into this power source (and meditation is a great way to do this), it's a question of staying connected.

As we know, it doesn't take much to steal our bandwidth and kick us off the feel-good grid. It's up to us to keep an eye on administrative protocol and prevent sneaky unauthorised users from hijacking our frequency. The good news? When we master the knack of switching from FOMO to JOMO, reconnecting with our happy medium is less of a balancing act and more of a seamless transition. And that's gotta mean something.

CHAPTER 7

Finding Meaning

How Connected are You?

It is quality rather than quantity that matters.

LUCIUS ANNAEUS SENECA, *ON SOPHISTICAL ARGUMENT*

E veryone has a number. It's not something that comes up in general conversation but we've all got one. In fact, it would probably shock most of us to learn just how many digits we've racked up over time. How does an average of 150 sound? Gobsmacked? Peeling the aul mandible off the floor? Look, before you start blaming those college years, there's really nothing to be ashamed of. We humans aren't equipped to deal with more than 150 active social connections. Gotcha! You were worried there for a minute, weren't you?

For the record: this isn't any arbitrary number. The theory, first proposed in the 1990s by British anthropologist and evolutionary psychologist Robin Dunbar, has been touted, tested and talked about, particularly since the onset of social media looked like it would scupper his big idea.

Here's the deal: most of us, depending on how sociable we are, can comfortably maintain regular stable relationships with between 100 and 200 people, the average being 150. Anything more than this requires an administrative crack team to enforce the rules of interaction and keep the natives from getting restless. Within this magic number is a series of layered relationships based on the strength of your ties. The first group, of 150, are your casual network (those you usually see at weddings and funerals). The next group, of 50, are your 'clan', or established social acquaintances (those you see regularly). The third group, of 15, are your confidantes (those who've got the dirt on you), and finally the smallest group, of five, are your tightest kemosabes (those you'd trust to hide the dirt) – usually a mix of friends and family. Over time, faces will vary and names will change, but the number remains the same. Why? We're limited by the size of our brains. If they were bigger, we'd be holding bigger parties.

And this is where it gets interesting. Our WiFi-enabled global village may potentially link us up to just about anyone in the world (hello, Oprah!), but it doesn't expand our ability to connect meaningfully beyond 150 people. In fact, it can potentially chip away at it. For example, if you spend more time following @justinbieber online than hanging out with your brother Justin, your brain will eventually file the Beebs as a closer contact than your sibling. Over time and with repetition, your top five could easily consist of people you know of but who wouldn't know you if you slapped their arses and called them sweetheart.

Liking and sharing updates with your extended social media family may feel rewarding (most positive reinforcements do) but over time, the lack of actual face-time (not to be confused with the app on your iPad) can make our connections less satisfying. Although debate is still ongoing regarding the effect of the internet on our social ties, one thing is undisputed: an online connection is not the same as an intimate in-person bond. Just ask Aristotle. He was the guy who said you could count your closest connections on one hand – in other words, Dunbar's five.

The bottom line? The more attention we pay to virtual connections, the less deep our real-life ones, and the less of them we have. The fewer real-life bonds we maintain, the more disconnected we become – not just from our social ties but from the sense of meaning these connections bring to our lives. Happy medium? Not so much. The goal of this chapter? To improve our connection speed by plugging into a more universal power supply. Interested? Let's find out more.

Problems, Passion and Purpose

Happiness comes from the intersection of what you love, what you're good at, and what the world needs.

OLIVER SEGOVIA, 'TO FIND HAPPINESS, FORGET ABOUT PASSION'

In order to feel connected to a greater power source, you need to figure out what gives you purpose and a sense of meaning. You don't need to be a member of an organised religion to feel connected to something bigger. You can believe in twerking aliens and magic mermaids if that's your jam, or you could make like Cher and believe in life after love – whatever gives you guidance and fills your value coffers. What is essential is that you consciously direct your attention outside of yourself, so that you don't turn into a narcissistic, self-absorbed sod. Harsh, I know, but there's a good reason for my acid tongue.

All the insignificant problems we complain about – no coconut milk in Starbucks; forgotten phone chargers; abysmal broadband speed – tend to go toodle-pip when we focus attention outside of ourselves. Remember Chapter 5? By swapping 'What am I getting out of this?' for an attitude of 'What am I putting into this?', we create the ideal circumstances for flow and well-being. Shifting our attention from 'me' to 'we' helps us share something of value and, in turn, create substance. Above all, we experience one of life's most delicious distractions – we forget about ourselves.

You see, happiness may be an inside job, but it finds its true value when applied to the outside world. Easier said than done, am I right? Wrong. Finding your purpose doesn't necessarily involve shamanic divination training or attending a Tibetan sound-healing ceremony. It's much simpler than that. In order to add soul to your goal, this 'something bigger' should tick the following boxes:

- It needs to be outside of your perceived capabilities.
- It needs to be for the good of others – your Dunbar connections and/or the community at large.
- You need to believe (however remotely) that you will achieve this goal. In other words, you need to be realistic and you need to have some grit, kiddo.

In combination, these dramatic elements provide the right amount of tension without making us tense; the right amount of drive without driving us to distraction; the right amount of compassion without holding a pity party. That's not to say you need to be a card-carrying member of Confucius' *junzi* club (*junzi* were akin to moral superheroes in ancient Chinese society) but having pure intentions, a mission if you will, connects your WiFi signal to both people and purpose.

Here's where it gets interesting. We could spend hours, days, years, a lifetime even, wondering what in the name of blazes this 'something bigger' is, where our true purpose lies, or we could, on the advice of Harvard Business Review journalist Oliver Segovia, swap passions for problems in our search for happiness.

'Putting problems at the centre of our decision-making changes everything,' notes Segovia in an article entitled 'To Find Happiness, Forget About Passion', which advocates looking into big issues that affect us personally to create more satisfaction in our lives.

Fair point. Focusing on global struggles can bring out the best in us, create character and lay the foundation for fulfilment in what we do. In the interests, however, of maintaining our happy medium, I'd like to suggest including smaller problems as well. These poor fellas tend to get overlooked, traded off as insignificant and not worth our attention, but they can be just as illuminating to our search for purpose.

Let's invite passion into the fold as well. Sure, passion gets a bad rap for being an over-ardent soul but with a little guidance, that burning desire can be used to create killer purpose follow-through, as illustrated by this simple equation.

The Three Ps

Problem (motivation) x Passion (follow-through) = Purpose (result)

What's inspired about this equation is how it synthesises both head (the problem that motivates us) and heart (our desire to fix it). Discovering the problem that motivates us uses our cognitive processes, while applying our passion to follow-through uses our emotions. The result? A mind–heart combination, a blend of thought and feeling – the essence of purpose. And that is where the magic happens!

Fun fact: in Chinese, the word for heart and mind is the same – *xin*.

Still not sure how your interest in vintage model trains benefits the greater good? Perhaps you're finding this whole passion rhetoric is a bit of a head-scratcher. Relax. I've got this. All you need is that notebook and pen. Leave the rest to me.

Making the Connection

The aim of this exercise is to create purpose from the inside out. By connecting the problems that motivate us with the passions that inspire us to action, we've got the potential to create more well-being in our day-to-day existence and to make a difference, whether large or small, to the world around us.

- Grab your notebook and pen and start by brainstorming the biggest problems that motivate you, both personally and globally, under the heading 'Problems'. These can be anything from civil rights activism to activating your glutes, cleaning up the ocean to cleaning up your closet. It's your call.

- Next, list your biggest passions under the heading 'Passions'. Whether it's Japanese clay modelling or catwalk modelling, Dungeons and Dragons role play or, ahem, a different kind of role play, allow your imagination to run wild (with passion). Don't be shy!

- Finally, under the heading 'Purpose', list any connections between the previous two columns, as these will help you figure out how your passions can impact the problems that affect you (directly or indirectly). Maybe there's a link between working the runway and advocating better working conditions for garment workers. Maybe your purpose is less public and more personal. I know folks who use hill-walking and forest treks as stress therapy and have inspired others in their immediate circle to do the same. Small steps count just as much along the middle path, so long as you're able to use your purpose to make an impact on the world around you.

While you're filling out your chart, how about I tell you a little story about the inspiration behind my first book, *The Happy Closet*? You know, while we're on the subject of passion-driven problem-solving and all?

Cluttered closet (motivation) x Fashion and mindfulness (follow-through) = Sartorial zen

The inspiration for *The Happy Closet* came from an intersection of passion meeting problems through which emerged my purpose – helping people transform their wardrobes from the inside out by decluttering the hang-ups and habits that shape our wardrobe wellness.

Here's the thing: I may be a fashion professional by trade, but I'm also a reformed hoarder by habit. For years, I lived with the irony (and attendant shame) of having a closet full of clothes and nothing to wear. I was an official card-carrying Impulse Buyer – a need-it-now shopper hooked on the thrill of the moment with little regard for the bigger picture, until it greeted me in the form of a whopping credit-card bill each month. Enter shame's evil twin – regret.

I sacrificed my own happy medium on the altar of fashion for years, dressing the person I thought I should be (big-shot influencer) instead of who I really was (wannabe big-shot influencer). I chose persona over purpose, appearance over authenticity, and fell foul of the consequences. Every time I opened my closet doors, I got a high-definition snapshot of personal insecurities, from my need for external validation (those 'ohs' and 'ahs' don't come cheap, you know!) to my desire to feel unique.

I knew that if I were to create long-term fashion flow (and not an avalanche each time I attempted getting dressed), I had to understand the hang-ups, driving the habits that were shaping my closet unhappiness. As on the outside, so on the inside. The result? This purposeful problem-solving did more than declutter my closet; it inspired me to create a system to help others identify their emotional hang-ups and habits and make more considered shopping choices rather than buying into hidden agendas and misplaced 'needs'. I turned my passion into a business, then converted it into a book to inspire readers to create fashion flow in their own time, on their own terms.

Check out my problem–passion–purpose chart on the next page to see how the pieces of the puzzle all fit.

PROBLEM	PASSION	PURPOSE
MOTIVATION	FOLLOW-THROUGH	RESULT
MIND	HEART	MIND–HEART
Fashion can tap into our personal insecurities and gathering tendencies, triggering us to buy what we don't want or need. ↓ This leads to both mental and physical clutter, and emotional baggage. ↓ The result? A closet full of clothes and nothing to wear.	Fashion Mindfulness Psychology Writing Coffee Cats	To create mindfulness techniques that help people find more purpose than potential in what they wear. ↓ To help people confront their inner hoarder and address the behaviours that lead to sartorial overwhelm. › ↓ To write a book that inspires others to create wardrobe wellness on their own terms.

As you can see from my chart, not every passion will hold hands with a problem (see: kitties and caffeine). Some might be too big for your present capacity management but stay connected to your ideas. Revisit them once in a while and see if you still feel the same way or simply reshape them to suit you now. You can still connect with people and with a greater purpose on a small scale. It's only small thinking that gets in the way of change.

My next mission? To start a cat café where punters can relax with a book, a flat white and a furry rescue friend. The cats get taken care of; the customers de-stress (in the words of St Francis of Assisi, 'a cat purring on your lap is more healing than any drug in the world'); and the option to adopt one of the whiskered wonders creates a beautiful symbiosis.

OK, my cat café idea may not be purr-fect (see what I did there?) as I have a history of cats high-tailing it and fur-saking me (sorry, shameless). With that said, I'm prepared to scale back on my pet passion (that's it, I promise) and opt for swapsies. I'll pony up the java and doughnuts if someone will let me cat-sit for them (feline Airbnb?). Everyone wins! Pet therapy. It's the future.

Wherever your passion-driven problem-solving mission leads you, remember one thing: what we do defines not only us but the world around us too, so make sure you're happy with the direction. The last thing you want is to look back a few years down the road and think, 'Well, that was a waste of time'. Your contribution doesn't have to be earth-shattering, award-winning or hall of fame-worthy – even small causes can have big effects. It just needs to add a plotline to your story, something that motivates you to take action and make a broader impact on the world around you – a living legacy, if you will.

The Happiness Legacy

We will be known forever by the tracks we leave.

NATIVE AMERICAN PROVERB

It's not often that I am at a loss for words. Speechlessness is something to be avoided in my line of work, so I always carry some spare colloquial change should I be caught short. Of course, the very day I could have used the dig-out, my mental pockets were empty. I sat there in front of a packed audience looking like I had been slapped in the gob with a mouldy turnip. Attractive. I had been asked to participate on a panel for a corporate International Women's Day event and damn was I excited. I had done the arithmetic of possible questions and how I would approach them: bridging the pay gap, breaking the glass ceiling, defining career success. My bases were covered – or so I thought. The MC asked me a very simple question to which I had absolutely no answer: 'What would you like your legacy to be?' Crickets. Tumbleweed. Radio silence. Cut to break. Cut to break! Only it was live and all sorts of awkward. 'I honestly don't know,' I conceded. It was the best I could do, given that most of the front row at this point were now personally acquainted with my dental work.

Sometimes the simplest questions are the most thought-provoking. In truth, I never thought of my life as something to be handed down. For so long, my story had been one of withstanding as opposed to outstanding. I was a bit late to the party when it came to finding my own happy medium and it most certainly didn't involve any extensive liquid assets to bequeath (unless you count my Butler's Cafe free coffee points). The more I thought about it, though, the more questioning my legacy started to make perfect sense. The question wasn't about my material achievements. It was more about how I wanted the story of my life to be told. My Oprah lightbulb moment had arrived! After the room has emptied, naturally.

Contrary to popular belief, a legacy isn't something we leave behind. We're all living our legacy – each and every one of us, each and every day, from the money we earn to the company we keep and how we choose to look at the world. Our endowment doesn't need to include a 21,000-square-foot penthouse or a couture collection to rival that of Daphne Guinness to be memorable. It all boils down to how, to what and to whom we allocate our attention.

Living a Legacy

Pay attention. It's all about paying attention. Attention is vitality. It connects you with others. It makes you eager. Stay eager.

SUSAN SONTAG, *VASSAR COLLEGE COMMENCEMENT ADDRESS*

Web advocate. Pop culture maven. Professional bacon fan. Avid communicator. Friendly music buff. Proud Twitter practitioner. Social media freak. Beer guru. Entrepreneur. Incurable puppy fan. Amateur thinker. Pop culture queen. Internet trailblazer. Terminal Tumblr fiend. Sloe gin evangelist. Friend of rescue animals everywhere. Irascible innovator. Coffee guru. Netflix fanatic. Chipotle chickadee. Infuriatingly humble motivational speaker. Part-time zombie hunter. Top-notch audiophile. Eater of burritos. Lovable rogue. Hardcore hipster. Lifelong pizza lover. Percy Pigs purveyor. Full-time philanthropist. Champagne campaigner. Cleavage activist. Hot-dog dilletante. Solitary surf bum. Galloping gourmand. International man of mystery. Unstoppable snail racer. Globetrotter extraordinaire. Follower of dreams. Border-control bluffer. Extraordinary oenophile. Culture vulture. Self-styled publicist. Venerable junk food junkie. Audacious taco blogger. Amateur haiku warrior. Criminally good-looking. Mendacious Nutella devotee. Marmite maniac. Brunch pugilist. Hardened hood rat. Unshakeable mamma's boy. Bona fide breast man. Moral hygiene habitué. Avid programme coder. Wannabe One Direction member. Irritating influencer. Peerless nap-taker. Aspiring actress. Kaiser of cool. Doer of nothing. Lover of life.

It's easy to make ourselves look fancy-pants on the web. All it takes is a thesaurus, some imagination and the ability to hold a straight face before pressing 'save' on that 160-character social media bio. Living up to it is a different story altogether.

You may want to be perceived as a tireless volunteer whose NGO work will go down in the annals of history, but if your social media footprint calls you out as a doer of aimless scrolling and liking what others have done, then it might be best to mind the gap before disembarking onto the delusional platform. Our old friend Aristotle had it right when he suggested the good life arises from doing what you say, rather than just saying what you do. In other words, actions speak louder than words. Remember: the internet never forgets. Ditto for your offline shenanigans.

Becoming more conscious of what we expect from our legacy (in other words, the impact we have on the world around us) helps us make good decisions, to be purposeful about who we spend time with and how we want our personal plot to unfold. In order to tell the story of our happy medium, it's crucial that we connect with a purpose we value so that when we allocate our attention, we do it regret-free.

On the next few pages are two exercises to put the living in our legacy and the extra in our ordinary. Here's how it rolls out: the ordinary decent human exercise uses random acts of kindness to improve our kinship with others; while the smallies exercise applies stream-of-consciousness writing to connect us to simple things that make life worth living. So far, so good. But wait. There's a catch! Both exercises require a month of your time. A month? A MONTH! Settle, petal. Here's why.

Mindfulness is just cheap talk unless you are prepared to give it a signature walk. Like any habit worth forming, repetition is key. Hate to break it to you but the commonly-held belief that it takes 21 days to form a habit is a myth. According to habit-meister James Clear, it takes a *minimum* of about 21 days and, according to a study carried out by Phillippa Lally and her research team at University College London, an average of 66 days. Factor in personal behaviour and this number can vary anywhere between 18 and 254 days. In the spirit of a happy medium, I suggest splitting the difference and calling it a month. Fair enough? Good. Time we get some brain-training underway.

Ordinary Decent Human

Warning: kindness is contagious and habit-forming and has serious side effects. Prolonged daily use leads to compassion, empathy and unlimited well-being. Symptoms may develop immediately after exposure. Proceed with care.

- Kindness is an instant connector.
- Kindness is anti-ageing.
- Kindness is viral and highly contagious.
- Kindness is intoxicating..

We are wired for kindness. It's in our DNA. Without it, we couldn't create communities or form the strong, fulfilling bonds that keep us connected. Kindness is also contagious, spreads like good news and is highly intoxicating, which is why we love it so much. Oh, and it's a proven anti-inflammatory that is linked to anti-ageing benefits. Could this be any better? Wait, there's more. According to research from Emory University, performing acts of kindness tickle the brain's pleasure and reward centre as much as if the good deed was done to us too, not just to the recipient. Clever, that. This soft, fluffy, endorphin-fuelled feeling is colloquially known as the 'helper's high'. You can thank dopamine for this, which, in fact, did us a solid by making kindness addictive. So not only is kindness an instant connector but it makes us look good *and* feel tipsy good? Not a bad CV.

What's more, (oh yes, there's more!) Professor of Psychology at the University of California, Riverside, Sonja Lyubomirsky has established that good deeds contribute directly to an increase in well-being. According to her 2005 study of random acts of kindness, it reportedly takes a minimum of one good deed a day to increase our satisfaction levels. This is a woman who's studied happiness for over 20 years, so I reckon she knows what's she's talking about.

With that in mind, we're going to indulge our ordinary decent human – the person in all of us who is capable of great acts of kindness in small but powerful doses. This, my friends, is a habit you won't want to kick.

The idea behind this exercise is simple: to convert our connections into bonds. Kindness, like an emotional adhesive, creates instant bonds with others by reducing affective distance. Think of it as a goodness glue. Only don't stick your fingers together – you'll be of no use to anyone. Let's get started, shall we?

For this exercise, you will need:

- A notebook, calendar or diary (online or offline) and a pen
- A month

- A willingness to step outside of your comfort zone.

The mission, should you choose to accept it, is to conduct a random act of kindness each day for a month, making sure to note the following:

- How you felt
- How the other person/people reacted (where relevant).

Similar to the going with the flow exercise in Chapter 5, the idea is to increase our well-being daily by making the small things count – with one exception. The caveat? It has to be for someone you don't know. Why? Well, it's not a huge stretch to be a good egg to our Dunbar five or those within our immediate sphere of influence (plus, chances are they'll repay the kindness). It's a different story entirely if we challenge our hero (that's you!) to take on a quest that tests his or her comfort zone, elicits no payback and is for the greater good.

The beauty of this? Doing the decent thing doesn't involve a grand gesture, just a courtesy. It doesn't mean you have to trawl the streets like a superhero looking for a damsel in distress; although if you want to don your bad-ass cape from Chapter 4, be my guest. For the record, I've got dibs on the telepathic tiara, so don't even think about it.

In as much as possible, plan not to plan. If you get to the end of the day and haven't reached your random act of kindness quota, purloin a quickie from the list on page 189 but don't make a habit of it – it defeats the whole 'random' purpose.

Random acts of kindness are just that – impromptu, unplanned, spontaneous. Even though we are consciously scheduling to complete one a day, the idea is that by the end of the month, those neuropathways will be well-trod with the footprint of good deeds. The result? Being kind will have become an automatic response – not just a tick on a 'to do' list.

While you're flexing your connective tissue, kindly refrain from sharing your big heart on Facebook. An ordinary decent human doesn't feel obliged to get a fist-bump emoji for every act of kindness. By all means, highlight eyewitness accounts of kindness conducted by others but keep yours on the QT. There's a big difference between a deed done good and a do-gooder.

Finally, at the end of the month, look back on your entries and answer the following:

- Did the process become more automatic/habitual as the month progressed?
- Did you find more opportunities to be kind as your practice strengthened?
- Do you feel more connected to the world around you?
- How does your current feeling of satisfaction compare with how you felt a month ago?
- Did you wear the cape? (Just kidding.)

Kindness is one of the easiest and most rewarding ways of turbo-charging our connection speed with others, so put on that cape, sunshine, and get moving. Need some inspiration?

Choose a random act of kindness from the list below and start spreading the compassion contagion!

Say something positive (online): It takes zero conscious awareness to click 'like' on a social media post. It takes a bit more attention, however, to leave a genuine comment. Not much for the PDA? See it as an anti-trolling device: it'll annoy the hell out of the haters.

Be the coffee fairy: Spot someone their morning latte in the coffee queue behind you. Paying it forward can feel weird but, if in doubt, remember: no one turns down free coffee. It's like putting Baby in a corner – totally uncool and punishable by the ghost of Johnny Castle.

Be totally Irish: Salute EVERYONE you meet – on the road, in the elevator, in the supermarket queue. Wave, smile, wink, nod, finger-twitch – whatever you're feeling. Throw in a 'Nice day', 'Grand soft day' or 'Grand day for drying' for extra brownie points!

Stealth cake-drops: Imagine waking up one morning to find a pile of pain au chocolat on your doorstep. That, in my sweet-toothed opinion, is the dream! On that note, why not leave an anonymous box of baked goods for a neighbour who could use some sweetness in their day? P.S. I am open to donations.

Pay a compliment: Everyone loves a compliment. Granted, we're not the best at accepting them ('This rag? I found it in a dumpster behind some crime scene tape'), but everyone enjoys an ego boost. When indulging in praise, opt to sprinkle rather than shower. No one wants to be soaked in obsequiousness, especially if it's by someone you don't really know.

Give stuff away: Remember the hedonic treadmill? The one where we wear ourselves out in the pursuit of more stuff? Here's a tip: give stuff away! Job-lot it online. Give it to charity. Donate treats for digs, like spare mattresses and toasters, to students in need of a dig-out. It's a good excuse to clear the psychic cobwebs and do a well-needed declutter. Do good. Feel better.

Kindness is like a more of a muscle than a virtue and can be improved with regular exercise. In order grow a habit, we've got to step outside our comfort zone and feel a small burn. Bulk up your well-being workout with this following tip. Make a list (List Maker, that's you!) of the courtesies you'd usually extend to others in the course of a day, whether that's opening a door for someone, giving a driver the right of way or taking in your neighbour's bins under the header 'Automatic Habits'. Beside that make another list entitled 'New Habits'. Think of different ways you can supersize those automatic habits and fire up those neuropathways. Turn a smile into a 'thank you', a 'thank you' into small talk, small talk into a meaningful conversation – just take it one small step further than you usually would.

You know, sometimes we don't realise how much we have to give until we start doling it out. Small but steady acts of kindness are powerful tools in reminding us how good we have it. The more small acts of kindness we share with others, the stronger our human connections and the more balance we give to our lives, not to mention all the feel-good memories we create. Picture this: the human brain is thought to be able to store 2.5 petabytes of memories (for comparison, 1.5 petabytes of data is equivalent to 10 billion photos stored on Facebook). The more positive memories we can create, the greater our capacity for feeling connected. Mindfulness in action! Who'd have thought it could take something so small? Speaking of which ...

The Smallies

Small moments can often be overlooked in favour of their broadcastable, Pinterest-worthy, envy-inducing, Insta-fabulous brethren, those moments that occur a handful of times during our earthly existence – if we're lucky. Smallies, on the other hand, happen more often than Kanye West's Twitter rants, albeit with less fanfare. Despite their unassuming demeanour (they rarely get a shout out or a hashtag), smallies deliver big time on satisfaction. As the old saying goes, 'It's always the quiet ones.' Let's see how they stack up:

- Smallies happen daily.
- Smallies defy expectation (in fact, we often take them for granted).
- Smallies add plotline to our stories.
- Smallies put the extra in our ordinary.

In summation: smallies rule. And by golly, it's time to start noticing them more. Here's how we can give them a heads up. One last time for the cheap seats, folks. Let's make this count!

For this exercise, you'll need:

- A notebook and a pen
- Some quiet time
- All the feels.

The Idea

Here's the plan: you're going to spend five to ten minutes a day, each day for an entire month, writing down the small things the make you happy. These can be anything from listening to Prince on full blast to that satisfied feeling after a meal someone else made. Easy, right? Sure. Mindfulness appears simple enough on paper until we're required to practice it daily – on paper. Like any habit worth forming, repetition is key. This one's a beauty, so stick with it.

The Setting

You don't need a picture-perfect view from a Victorian bay window, a cat to curl around your feet or an Art Deco bone-china tea-set with dainty little macaroons to set the scene. That, my dear, is someone's Pinterest board. 'A room of one's own', as mandated by Virginia Woolf, is the ideal writing setting. Failing that, any quiet space should do the job nicely. By the way, now would be the perfect opportunity to enforce the 'no'-fly zone from Chapter 6.

The Method

Start by getting your five senses in on the gig. List all the little things you love according to what you can taste, touch, see, hear or smell. This will get your creative juices flowing until you can riff stream-of-consciousness style.

For the record: stream of consciousness isn't any fancy-schmancy mindfulness tool; it's merely a byword for moment-to-moment awareness of your immediate experience. Add a pen and some paper into the mix and it becomes a safety net for the smallies that get lost in life's shuffle.

Some friendly advice:

- Don't be afraid to give logic the heave-ho (again!) and let intuition do her thing.
- Don't spell-check, edit or nit-pick.
- Don't second-guess your thoughts or stop to involve the grammar police.

Just allow the brain to declutter and decompress. I guarantee you will be surprised with what it decides to deliver. Here's why.

The Science Bit

The physical act of getting things down on paper stimulates a collection of cells in the base of the brain known as the RAS (reticular activating system). This fine piece of machinery acts as a conduit for all the data your brain needs to process. In order to do its job, it focuses its attention squarely on whatever you're doing. The result? Distraction-free thinking and supercharged flow. Oh, yeah! Think of it as a Juno Instagram filter – including it in your mindfulness arsenal will add definition, intensity and brightness and will illuminate the subject at hand. Nice.

The Result

Now for the juicy bit. At the end of the month, review your notes and see if you can spot any patterns. Generally speaking, these are the smallies that mean the most to you. Not that any parent plays favourites but sometimes there are a few little fellas that give us all the feels. Sweet, eh? Read them whenever you have a 'poor me' moment or, for that matter, if you just want to power up that connection to something bigger. Feeling inspired? Keep adding to your list until you've created a book of beautiful moments. Need some inspiration? Why not check out my favourite smallies on the next page,

At this stage, you should be feeling a power surge, as if you've plugged into the universal grid. This feeling means something. In fact, it means a lot. By discovering those small things that give you satisfaction along with your individual narrative powers, you'll be able to find the story you were searching for all along – the warm highlights of that high-def, vibrant, vignette-edged, super-saturated life that you mistook for mere pleasantries instead of plot. Connect only with novelty or what's trending and you'll never find what truly satisfies. Plug into these small beauties instead and you won't feel the pressure of having it all – because, let's face it, you already do. It's right there on paper. This, my friend, is a legacy in itself. This is the magic we all seek. *This* is your happy medium.

Annmarie's Smallies

the feel of crisp sheets

surprising someone with a present

the hours ~~lost~~ gained to a great conversation

those few minutes of silence before the sun comes up

a glass of wine (or three) with friends on a weekend afternoon

family barbeques in my mother's garden

the collective euphoria (and spike in ice-cream sales) on a sunny day in Ireland

the intense toe-curling climax of a great suspense novel

the 'I can't believe that just happened!' feeling

the first sip of freshly brewed coffee

the sound of a baby's giggles

being breathless with laughter

flying above the clouds in a plane

seeing friends after too long

the smell of fresh air on someone's skin when they come inside from the cold

the mental clarity (and awesome tidiness) from decluttering

signing for an unexpected parcel

listening to 'Driving Home for Christmas' while ~~driving~~ being driven home for Christmas

snuggling my sister's pug

playing Frustration with my niece

cheeky naps

cats – always cats

CHAPTER 8

Happily Ever After

Retelling Your Story

There's always a story. It's all stories, really. The sun coming up every day is a story. Everything's got a story in it. Change the story, change the world.

TERRY PRATCHETT, *A HAT FULL OF SKY*

Well, look at you! You've become quite the hero, haven't you? A reluctant one perhaps but it's not as if this journey has been an easy one. That said, one often has to go to the edges to get back to the middle.

Let's recap on the action, shall we?

You took on weapons of mass distraction, dismantled limbic alarm bells and disposed of the toxic build-up from frequent gadget use without missing a beat. You captured the attention thieves, digital delinquents and dopamine dealers that tried scrambling your GPS signal, not to mention the Humble Braggers and sneaky Name Droppers who consistently photobombed your time-out. You enforced tight patrols on your 'no'-fly zone – boundaries that allow you to serve the community. And don't think those random acts of kindness went unnoticed. Most of all, you created a life on your terms – the good life. It looks, my friend, like you're Grand Grand Grand. Well, there you have it. I guess my work is done.

Before I take my expertly inexpert leave, we've got one order of business left. In order to maintain a happy medium, it helps to have a set of guidelines to keep us on the good foot, lest you start comparing your journey with that of others and forget who you really are. Consider it your personal happiness credo – 12 simple truths of well-being that'll keep you on the middle path, even amid life's many speed-bumps and wobbles. Find the verge in the verbiage and give yourself a breather. You deserve it.

The 12 Steps to a Happy Medium

1. Decide to be Satisfied

Can't get no satisfaction? Perhaps you're trying too hard to be happy. Ease off the elbow grease and take a breather, why don't you? Start by learning to be satisfied. Satisfaction is calmer, less intense and easy to achieve. It doesn't set impossibly high standards for itself and others which makes life a lot more enjoyable. Master the art of having enough instead of having it all and you'll never be happier. Now that's bound to be satisfying.

2. Ditch the Distractions

In order to make satisfying choices, you've got to decide what's worth your attention. If you're constantly preoccupied with the nagging of your smartphone, what others are doing and lists of 'to dos' that don't need to be done, you'll never stay focused enough to understand what we need. The middle ground is your distraction firewall. With it, your attention is protected from spurious incoming interruptions; without it, it's vulnerable to being phished right from under your nose.

3. Connect IRL

Ah, our WiFi-enabled global village – ain't it cosy? For as connected and close as we all feel (put the kettle on, @jk_rowling!), we could all do with a bit more human-to-human interaction. The irony of modern life? The more we focus on our online connections, the more disconnected we become from our real-life bonds. Happy medium? Not so much. The trick? To blend rather than blur the lines between our online and offline tribes. Seriously, someone put on the kettle. I take my tea very seriously.

4. Accept Your Selfie

Selfie culture is here to stay. As long as the front-facing camera phone is pointed in your direction, the question will always remain 'Why?' Approval by committee rarely serves the individual, even if the consensus is a thumbs-up. One hundred likes may give your ego a much-loved boost but when you rely on the validation of others to cushion your self-esteem, then, Houston, we've got a problem. Accepting your selfie is the first step to curbing compulsive comparison and curbing the tendency to imitate water-fowl. Do the ducks a favour.

5. Show Some Gratitude

So you don't have a multi-million euro recording deal, a prime-time reality show or Colin Farrell on speed dial. Most of us don't. What's worth your consideration is what you already have. A simple shift in perspective and an added dose of gratitude can help you learn to be happy with who and where you are right now. Look around you and give the Oscar speech of your life. Thank your parents, your agent, your solicitor, your pet poodle, the 1,000-thread count duvet on your bed, Marks & Spencer for their weekend meal deals – the choice is yours. Just make like Halle Berry and don't stop because, let's face it, no one's going to toss you off the stage. You get to be the winner every day – that choice is yours too.

6. Go with the Flow

Life's road blocks and traffic jams getting you down? Why don't you take the path of least resistance? Oh, I see – because it's too easy. There's got to be a catch, right? Wrong. Finding cruise-control allows for flow, which lifts the barriers and tolls imposed on our attention spans, ensuring a rapid passage to personal satisfaction. By incorporating time-expanding activities into your day-to-day living, you can learn to crowd out distraction, increase the quality of your attention and, in turn, make better choices. Allow your natural strengths and resources to take you where you want to be instead of girding your loins for gridlock. You'll be glad you did.

7. Unplug

No WiFi? No problem. There's a big difference between staying connected and forming bonds, retrieving information and using your intuition to understand things that bit deeper. Asking Siri about the meaning of life instead of using your own nous isn't going to make you any happier. Becoming too reliant on technology can lead you to lose your internal WiFi (wisdom, intuition, feelings, instinct) signal – the very qualities that keep you tuned in and turned on to what really matters.

8. Reframe FOMO

Perspective is a mighty mindfulness tool. Think of it as an Instagram filter. Too much glare? Slap a Mayfair on that squint-fest and suddenly life looks brighter and sharper. Click on the dreaded Walden and life becomes a whole lot colder. A different light is all it takes to see things differently and reframe missed opportunities as deliberate decisions. Establishing scheduling boundaries frees you up to concentrate on what's most important. By becoming more conscious of what you expect from your time, you're better positioned to make easier decisions about how to use it and manage the lingering fear of missing out. It's up to you to decide what makes the cut.

9. Learn to Love Problems

If you genuinely want to experience happiness, then get familiar with your problems. Court them. Take them out for a drink. Be a good listener and by all means hear what they're saying instead of gossiping about them or, worse, ignoring them. If you're really clever, you'll see how you can help others in the same situation. If you're really lucky, you'll find an unexpected connection to your passion.

10. Pursue Potential with Purpose

We all have potential. How we choose to deploy it is what creates purpose. Sometimes you've got a talent that's worth exploring; sometimes you can only take it so far. It's up to you to understand where to draw the line and focus your attention elsewhere. If chasing your dream is making you sick, broke, exhausted or annoying to be around, then maybe it's time to call time. The beauty of potential? There's a lot more where that came from. Be open to exploring other options.

11. Embrace Life's In-Betweens

Finding meaning in life doesn't entail embarking on an *Eat, Pray, Love* excursion to south-east Asia or joining a womb circle in the Andes (unless of course, you want to); rather it's about reconnecting with the everyday bliss bringers that lend a soft lens and gentle scent of gardenia to even the most humble tasks. You know it as that pocket of sunshine your cat invariably seems to find, the moment of silence before your children wake up and the day officially begins. This is where you are truly satisfied; this is where happiness *actually* lives.

12. Live Your Legacy

Imagine if you only had a month left on the earth. How would you fill those 30 days? Would you donate your worldly possessions to charity, stage a naked protest, take a bath in a Nebuchadnezzar of 1999 Bollinger La Gran Annee Brut? Maybe you'd give that Silicon Valley TEDTalk like you always dreamed or get hitched in Vegas by an Elvis impersonator. Perhaps. Once you'd kicked the bucket-list, you'd most likely spend time with family and friends, doing the things that soothe your soul. Whatever your preference, remember: grand gestures may add special effects to our stories but it's the small moments of presence, how we connect with others that establish a solid plotline.

Time's up, folks. It's over to you. By now you should feel like an active agent in your own story. You've done all the hard graft so it's time to kick back and enjoy the view. If you've got a beverage handy, now would be the time to raise a toast.

Here's to navigating choice, marshalling attention and ditching those digital distractions. Here's to separating selfies from your authentic self and learning to go beyond face value. Here's to facing up to FOMO, establishing boundaries and learning how to say 'no' like a pro.

Here's to following your instincts and not following the herd. Here's to finding your strengths and going with the flow. Here's to killing comparisons, eliminating excessive expectations and developing an attitude of gratitude. Here's to a life more ordinary – and so more extraordinary. Most of all, here's to you.

Welcome to your happy medium – this is your story, so tell it like it is.

Yours,

Annmarie x

GLOSSARY OF TERMS

404 Error: An error message/web page generated by a website-hosting server when a user attempts to follow a broken or dead link.

Animated gif: An animated image of twerking cats, fist-bumps, facepalms or eye-rolls, compressed to reduce transfer time. 'Gif' stands for graphics interchange format. In the land of 140-characters, one image says it all.

Click-bait: Internet content of an especially provocative or sensational nature whose main intention is to attract visitors or draw people to the web page. See also: sticky.

Cyberslacking: Using the internet to look productive during work hours while booking flights for a weekend city break.

Distractify: An oxymoronic portmanteau of 'distract' and 'satisfy'. Also, a leading entertainment company that 'wants wasting time to be more than just of a waste of time'.

Egosurfing: The practice of Googling one's own name in order to review the results.

FaceBragging: Using Facebook as a platform to post self-congratulatory updates of one's own life. For example: *My* *amazing boyfriend surprised me today with a Birkin bag! I never realised he was so connected. Hope it doesn't get too wet on our yacht trip around the Maldives.* Often accompanied by a bang of false humility.

FaceStalking: Using Facebook to repeatedly check someone's profile page, relationship status, pictures and who they've been speaking to. Often obtained without their knowledge. Commonly considered light stalking.

Fauxcellarm: A portmanteau of 'faux' and 'alarm'. Used to describe the weird sensation of your mobile phone vibrating even when you are not carrying it. See also: phantom limb; ringxiety.

FOMO (Fear of Missing Out): An acronym used to describe the low-level anxiety experienced when witnessing the social rewards enjoyed by others.

Google Hangouts: The online equivalent of the work watercooler but with video chat and instant messaging.

Hot-dog legs: A term used to describe a social media shot of one's tanned legs from the vista of a beach deck-chair. Frequently used to instigate FOMO in others.

Hyperlink: A highlighted word or set of words designed to take you to another page. Acts as a dangling carrot of distraction.

IRL: An internet acronym for In Real Life. Often used to distinguish life online from that offline.

Klout Score: An online ~~metric~~ popularity contest designed to establish the quorum of one's social media influence.

JOMO (Joy of Missing Out): An acronym used to describe self-imposed social exclusion and deliberate downtime.

LinkedIn: Facebook for business networking. Also a legit excuse to get one's social networking fix during work hours.

Mayfair: A popular Instagram filter boasting warm pink tones that has the potential to instantly erase the evidence of a hangover.

Meme: An image, video or piece of text, typically humorous in nature, copied and spread rapidly by internet users, often with slight variations. See also: animated gif.

Nomophobia: A neologism comprised of the words 'no', 'mobile' and 'phobia'. Used to describe the fear of being without one's mobile phone.

Phantom limb: The sensation that an amputated or missing limb is still attached to the body and moving appropriately with other body parts.

Phubbing: The act of snubbing someone by paying attention to your phone. Socially permissible in groups of three or more; a red flag on a date or any one-on-one situations.

Ringxiety: A portmanteau of 'ring' and 'anxiety'. The perception that one's mobile phone is vibrating or ringing when it is not. See also: fauxcellarm; phantom limb.

Save as: A prompt to save a version of a file on a hard drive.

Sticky: Priority boarding and a first-class upgrade for an online thread. Usually a topic of interest to users (i.e. distracting) that will get them to stay and travel around the specific website on which it is posted. See also: click-bait.

TMI: An acronym for 'too much information'. Often used to describe inappropriate levels of self-disclosure in person or online. For example: *That blog post about Amy's turbo colon cleanse was a bit TMI, don't you think?*

Toggle: To click back and forth between pages. A thinly-disguised ploy to make one feel productive.

TOGO: Short for 'tired of going out'. See also: JOMO.

TOGOAMOOSI: Short-ish for 'tired of going out and missing out on staying in'. See also: JOMO.

Tumblr: A micro-blogging/social networking platform used primarily by teenagers, kidults and amateur porn enthusiasts.

Vine: A 6-second video clip often used to share a slice of life.

Viral: (of an image, video, piece of information, etc.) Circulated rapidly and widely from one internet user to another. Quickly or widely spread, popularised from person-to-person electronically micro-blogging. See also: meme.

Walden: A not-so-popular Instagram filter, due to its yellowish tinge. Kiss of death for selfies.

WiFi: Oxygen.

Wiki: Not to be confused with a Wookie; a website or database developed collaboratively by a community of users, allowing any user to add and edit content.

FURTHER READING

Amin, Amit. 'The 31 Benefits of Gratitude You Didn't Know About: How Gratitude Can Change Your Life.' Happier Human: What About Happiness? (http://happierhuman.com/benefits-of-gratitude/).

Andrews, Sally, David A. Ellis, Heather Shaw and Lukasz Piwek. 'Beyond Self-Report: Tools to Compare Estimated and Real-World Smartphone Use.' *PLoS ONE* 10.10 (October 2015).

Aristotle. *The Nicomachean Ethic* (trans. David Ross, ed. Lesley Brown). Oxford University Press, 2009.

Berdik, Chris. *Mind Over Mind: The Surprising Power of Expectations.* Penguin, 2013.

Burke, Moira, Cameron Marlow and Thomas Lento. 'Social Network Activity and Social Well-Being.' Proceedings of the SIGCHI Conference on Human Factors in Computing Systems, Association for Computing Machine, 2010.

Carr, Nicholas. *The Shallows: How the internet is changing the way we think, read and remember.* Atlantic Books, 2010.

Clear, James. www.jamesclear.com.

Csikszentmihalyi, Mihaly. 'Flow, the secret to happiness.' TED2004, 2004 (https://www.ted.com/talks/mihaly_csikszentmihalyi_on_flow#t-197278).

Czerwinski, Mary, Edward Cutrell and Eric Horvitz. 'Instant Messaging and Interruption: Influence of Task and Type on Performance.' OzCHI 2000 Conference Proceedings, 2000.

Dar Meshi, Diana and Hauke R. Heekeren Tamir. 'The Emerging Neuroscience of Social Media.' *Trends in Cognitive Sciences* 19.12 (December 2015).

Dash, Anil. 'JOMO!' Anildash.com (http://anildash.com/2012/07/jomo.html).

Desan, Paul, Dan Tomasulo, Stefan Goldfinch, Debra Park and Mark Setton. The Pursuit of Happiness (www.pursuit-of-happiness.org)

Dienstmann, Giovanni. 'Types of Meditiation: An Overview of 23 Meditation Techniques.' Live and Dare (http://liveanddare.com/types-of-meditation/).

Dobelli, Rolf. *The Art of Thinking Clearly: Better Thinking, Better Decisions.* Sceptre, 2013.

Dolan, Paul. *Happiness by Design: Finding Pleasure and Purpose in Everyday Life.* Penguin, 2015.

Duhigg, Charles. *Smarter Faster Better: The Secrets of Being Productive.* William Heinemann, 2016.

— *The Power of Habit: Why We Do What We Do and How to Change.* William Heinemann, 2012.

Dunbar, R.I.M. 'Neocortex size as a constraint on group size in primates.' *Journal of Human Evolution* 22.6 (June 1992).

Fake, Caterina. 'Fomo and Social Media.' Caterina.net (https://caterina.net/2011/03/15/fomo-and-social-media/).

Fey, Tina. *Bossypants.* Sphere, 2011.

Gaffney, Maureen. *Flourishing: How to achieve a deeper sense of well-being, meaning and purpose – even when facing adversity.* Penguin, 2011.

Gilbert, Daniel. *Stumbling on Happiness.* Harper Perennial, 2006.

Goffman, Erving. *The Presentation of Self in Everyday Life.* Anchor, 1959.

Haidt, Jonathan. *The Happiness Hypothesis: Putting Ancient Wisdom and Philosophy to the Test of Modern Science*. Arrow, 2006.

Hanson, Rick. 'How to Trick Your Brain for Happiness.' Greater Good: The Science of a Meaningful Life (http://greatergood.berkeley. edu/article/item/how_to_trick_your_brain_for_happiness).

Huffington, Arianna. *Thrive: The Third Metric to Redefining Success and Creating a Happier Life*. W.H. Allen, 2014.

Iyer, Pico. 'The Art of Stillness in the Digital Age.' Wisdom 2.0 (http:// wisdom2conference.com/videos/myriad_single_element/1812).

Kahneman, Daniel. *Thinking Fast and Slow*. Penguin, 2012.

Konikova, Maria. 'The Limits of Friendship.' *The New Yorker*, 7 October 2014.

Kramer, Adam D. I., Jamie E. Guillory and Jeffrey T. Hancock. 'Experimental evidence of massive-scale emotional contagion through social networks.' *PNAS* 111.23 (June 2014).

Lally, Phillippa, Cornelia H.M. van Jaarsveld, Henry W.W. Potts and Jane Wardle. 'How habits are formed: Modelling habit formation in the real world.' *European Journal of Social Psychology* 40.6 (2010).

Liu, Yingzhao. 'Buddhist Alchemy: Transforming Everything into Wisdom.' Wisdom 2.0 (http://wisdom2conference.com/Videos/ myriad_single_element/2385).

Marche, Stephen. 'Is Facebook Making Us Lonely?' *The Atlantic*, May 2012.

Mascaro, Jennifer S., Alana Darcher, Negi T. Lobsand and Charles L. Raisonand. 'The neural mediator of kindness-based meditation: a theoretical model.' *Frontiers in Psychology* 6 (March 2015).

Masicampo, E.J. and and Roy F. Baumeister. 'Toward a Physiology of Dual-Process Reasoning and Judgment: Lemonade, Willpower, and Expensive Rule-Based Analysis.' *Psychological Science* 19.3 (March 2008).

— 'Consider It Done! Plan Making Can Eliminate the Cognitive Effects of Unfulfilled Goals.' *Journal of Personality and Social Psychology* 101.4 (October 2011).

McGonigal, Kelly. *Maximum Willpower: How to Master the Science of Self-Control*. Macmillan, 2012.

McLeod, S.A. 'Cognitive Dissonance.' SimplyPsychology (http://www. simplypsychology.org/cognitive-dissonance.html).

O'Connor, Annmarie. *The Happy Closet: Well-being is Well-dressed*. Gill Books, 2015.

Puett, Michael and Christine Gross-Loh. *The Path: A New Way to Think about Everything*. Viking, 2016.

Rutledge, Pamela. '8 Ways Selfies Can Make Your Life Better.' The Media Psychology Blog (http://mprcenter.org/blog/2014/01/8-ways-selfies-can-make-your-life-better/).

Schwartz, Barry. *The Paradox of Choice: Why More is Less*. HarperCollins, 2004.

Segovia, Oliver. 'To Find Happiness, Forget About Passion'. Harvard Business Review (https://hbr.org/2012/01/to-find-happiness-forget-about).

Seligman, Martin. *Authentic Happiness: Using the New Positive Psychology to Realize Your Potential for Lasting Fulfillment*. Nicholas Brealey Publishing, 2003.

Seppälä, Emma. *The Happiness Track: How to Apply the Science of Happiness to Accelerate Your Success*. Piaktus, 2016.

Sethi Lokanksha. 'Social Media Addiction: 39,757 Years Of Our Time Is Collectively Spend On Facebook In A Day!' DazeInfo (http://dazeinfo.com/2015/01/12/social-mdia-addiction/).

Simon, H.A. 'Rational Choice and the Structure of the Environment.' *Psychological Review* 63.2 (March 1956).

Spitzer, Manfred. *Digitale Demenz: Wie wir uns und unsere Kinder un der Verstand bringen.* Droemer HC, 2012.

Tsang, Jo-Ann. Carpenter, Thomas P. Roberts, James A. Frisch, Michael B. Carlisle, Robert D. 'Why are materialists less happy? The role of gratitude and need satisfaction in the relationship between materialism and life satisfaction.' *Personality and Individual Differences* 64 (July 2014)

Van Dyk, Spencer. 'Human sare only able to maintain five relationships in their inner circle, 150 in their outer circle: study.' *National Post*, 3 May 2016.

Ware, Nat. 'Why we're unhappy – the expectation gap.' TEDxKlagenfurt, 2014 (http://tedxtalks.ted.com/video/Why-we-re-unhappy-the-expectati).

Winfrey, Oprah. *What I Know For Sure.* Macmillan, 2014.

Wolf, Naomi. *The Beauty Myth.* Random House, 1990.